To every soul that has searched for truth and found peace in Islam, this book is for you. To those who embraced the light despite challenges, may Allah strengthen your faith and fill your heart with tranquility. To the new Muslims navigating this journey, you are never alone—Allah's mercy is always with you. And to those who guided, supported, and welcomed reverts with kindness, may Allah reward you abundantly. This book is a testament to the beauty of Islam and the journey of faith.

THE PATH TO
ISLAM
A GUIDE FOR NEW MUSLIM

———— ◇ ————

A Comprehensive Guide to Faith, Worship, and Daily Life in Islam

TAWHEED PUBLICATIONS

"And whoever Allah guides—he is the rightly guided; and whoever He sends astray—you will never find for them protectors besides Him." (Surah Al-Kahf 18:17)

Islam is a journey of the heart, mind, and soul, guided by the mercy of Allah. For every seeker who found the path of truth, this verse serves as a reminder that guidance is a gift from the Most Merciful. Embracing Islam is not the end, but the beginning of a lifelong journey toward light, wisdom, and peace.

Tawheed Publications

Contents

Foreword

In the name of Allah, the Most Gracious, the Most Merciful.

It is with great honor and joy that I introduce *The Path to Islam: A Guide for New Muslims* to those who have embraced Islam and those who are seeking to learn more about this beautiful faith. Becoming a Muslim is not merely a change in belief, but a profound spiritual transformation that requires dedication, patience, and a sincere desire to draw closer to Allah. This book has been written with the intention of providing new Muslims with the knowledge, tools, and support they need to navigate their new path and understand the depth and beauty of their faith.

In this book, you will find practical guidance on the five pillars of Islam, the essentials of worship, the teachings of the Quran, and the examples set by our beloved Prophet Muhammad ﷺ. These teachings, while deeply rooted in history, offer timeless wisdom for living a life of peace, purpose, and connection with the Creator. This guide is designed to help you understand the foundations of Islam, begin your journey of worship, and navigate the challenges that may arise as you adjust to a new way of life.

Becoming a Muslim is a journey, one that is both personal and collective. Along this path, you will encounter moments of joy, struggles, and growth. You will find comfort and solace in the words of the Quran and the Sunnah of Prophet Muhammad ﷺ, who exemplified kindness, patience, and wisdom. Remember, this journey is not about perfection; it is about striving for sincerity and making progress, no matter how small.

As you begin to implement what you learn in this book, know that you are not alone. You are part of a vibrant and diverse global community of believers. Seek support from fellow Muslims, and take time to deepen your understanding of Islam through prayer, reflection, and continuous learning.

Above all, trust in the mercy of Allah, who is always near to His servants, ready to guide, forgive, and support.

May Allah make your journey of faith filled with light, peace, and steadfastness. May He bless you with the strength to uphold His commandments and the wisdom to navigate life's challenges. And may He grant you success in this world and the Hereafter.

With prayers for your success and guidance,

Tawheed Publications

Preface

This book is a humble attempt to guide and support those who have embraced Islam and are now beginning a journey of profound transformation. The decision to accept Islam is one of the most significant decisions a person can make in their life. It is a decision to follow the straight path, seeking the guidance of Allah and striving to live according to His will.

When I first embarked on this journey, I encountered many questions, uncertainties, and challenges. I was filled with a deep sense of awe and wonder at the beauty of Islam, but also, at times, felt overwhelmed by the changes it required in my life. The need for a reliable guide was clear, one that would explain the essential aspects of Islam in a way that was practical and easy to understand.

This book is born out of that need. It is a comprehensive resource for new Muslims, written with simplicity and clarity, to help you better understand the core tenets of the faith and how to integrate them into your life. Whether you are taking your first steps in Islam or you have already begun your journey, this book will serve as a valuable tool in your quest for knowledge and spiritual growth.

In these pages, you will find guidance on the most essential aspects of Islam, from the foundational beliefs to the daily practices that will draw you closer to Allah. The chapters cover topics such as the Five Pillars of Islam, prayer, fasting, the importance of charity, and how to cultivate a meaningful relationship with Allah. You will also find reflections on the challenges that many reverts face and how to overcome them with patience, faith, and the support of the Muslim community.

Islam is a faith that calls to peace, mercy, and balance. It is a way of life that connects you with your Creator and provides you with a sense of purpose and direction. It offers practical solutions to the challenges of life, guidance for building strong relationships, and a path to spiritual fulfillment. The more you learn and understand about Islam, the more you will come to appreciate its beauty and wisdom.

As you read this book, I encourage you to take your time. There is no rush in this journey. Islam is not about achieving perfection overnight; it is about striving to improve each day and seeking closeness to Allah. This book is not just a collection of facts and practices—it is a journey in itself, one that invites you to reflect, grow, and deepen your faith.

I pray that Allah, in His infinite mercy, makes this book a source of benefit for you and that it helps you navigate the challenges and joys of being a new Muslim. May He guide you, protect you, and grant you success in this world and the Hereafter.

With sincere prayers for your success,

Tawheed Publications

Acknowledgments

I would like to express my deepest gratitude to all those who have supported me in the creation of this book. First and foremost, I thank Allah, the Almighty, for His guidance, mercy, and wisdom. Without His help, this book would not have come to fruition. It is through His grace that I have been able to write and share this work with those who seek knowledge about Islam.

I would also like to extend my heartfelt thanks to the many teachers, scholars, and fellow Muslims who have guided me along my own journey of faith. Their wisdom, patience, and encouragement have been invaluable, and their teachings continue to inspire and shape my understanding of Islam every day. I am forever grateful for their support and dedication.

To my family and friends, thank you for your constant love, encouragement, and understanding. Your patience during the times of research and writing has been truly appreciated, and your belief in this project kept me going even through moments of doubt.

I am especially grateful to the Muslim community around the world, whose kindness, generosity, and willingness to share their knowledge with others have provided me with the motivation to write this book. Their collective efforts in spreading the message of Islam, offering support to reverts, and creating spaces of learning have inspired me to contribute in whatever way I can.

Lastly, I would like to thank the countless reverts and new Muslims who have shared their personal stories, challenges, and triumphs. Your experiences have taught me so much about resilience, faith, and the beauty of the journey you have undertaken. May Allah reward you abundantly for your sincerity and perseverance.

May Allah accept this work from me and grant it benefit to those who read it. I pray that it serves as a source of guidance, comfort, and knowledge for all who seek it.

With heartfelt thanks,

Tawheed Publications

Prologue

Embarking on the journey of Islam is one of the most profound and transformative experiences a person can undertake. It is a path that leads to inner peace, spiritual growth, and closeness to Allah. For those who have embraced Islam, it marks the beginning of a new chapter in their lives, where the search for meaning, purpose, and direction finally finds its true home. This book is designed to be a companion to you on this journey—whether you are a new Muslim, someone seeking to better understand Islam, or someone who simply wants to deepen their connection with the faith. It is a guide to help you navigate the challenges, understand the principles, and find strength in the wisdom of Islam. Through this book, I hope to provide not only knowledge but also inspiration, comfort, and encouragement. The road ahead may be long, but with Allah's guidance and mercy, every step you take brings you closer to His light. I invite you to read with an open heart, reflecting on each lesson, and applying it to your life. May this book serve as a reminder that no matter where you are on your journey, Allah is always with you.

Introduction

Welcome to Islam – A New Beginning

Congratulations on embracing Islam! This moment marks the beginning of a beautiful journey—one that will bring you closer to your Creator, provide clarity about life's purpose, and introduce you to a global family of over a billion Muslims. You are now part of a tradition that spans centuries, a faith rooted in the pure monotheism preached by all prophets, from Adam to Noah, Abraham, Moses, Jesus, and finally, Muhammad ﷺ.

Embracing Islam is not just about reciting the Shahada (the testimony of faith); it is a transformation of the heart, mind, and soul. It is natural to feel a mix of emotions—excitement, joy, and perhaps even uncertainty about what comes next. You might be wondering how to begin practicing, how to explain your decision to others, or how to navigate challenges. Rest assured, you are not alone. Millions have walked this path before you, and there is an entire community eager to support you.

Allah tells us in the Quran:

> "Indeed, those who have said, 'Our Lord is Allah' and then remained steadfast—the angels will descend upon them, [saying], 'Do not fear and do not grieve but receive good tidings of Paradise, which you were promised.'" (Surah Fussilat 41:30)

Islam is a journey, not a destination. You do not need to know everything overnight. Take things step by step, and trust that Allah sees your sincerity and efforts. This book is designed to be your guide, answering your questions and helping you ease into your new life as a Muslim. Remember, every challenge you face is an opportunity for growth, and every step you take towards Allah brings you closer to His mercy and love.

My Journey to Islam – Understanding the Transition

Every revert to Islam has a unique and deeply personal journey. Some find Islam through years of studying different religions, while others experience a sudden realization that Islam is the truth. Perhaps you were inspired by the Quran's profound wisdom, the kindness of Muslim friends, or the peace you felt when learning about Islamic teachings. Whatever brought you to Islam, your journey is special and meaningful.

However, transitioning to a new faith comes with its own set of challenges. You may feel overwhelmed by the changes in lifestyle, such as learning how to pray, understanding what is halal and haram, or dealing with family and friends who might not understand your decision. It is important to know that these struggles are normal and part of the process. The Prophet Muhammad ﷺ himself reassured new Muslims, saying:

> **"Verily, this religion is easy, and whoever overburdens himself in his religion will not be able to continue in that way. So do not be extremists, but try to be near to perfection and receive the good tidings." (Sahih al-Bukhari)**

Islam is a religion of balance and gradual progress. You do not have to be perfect overnight. Start with the basics—strengthening your belief in Allah, learning to pray, and reading about the Prophet ﷺ. Give yourself time to grow spiritually and emotionally. You will make mistakes, but that is part of learning. What matters most is your sincerity and dedication to improving each day.

Surround yourself with supportive Muslim friends, seek knowledge, and trust that Allah will make your path easy. The Quran promises:

"And whoever fears Allah—He will make for him a way out and
will provide for him from where he does not expect."
(Surah At-Talaq 65:2-3)

This book will help guide you through this transition, providing practical advice, spiritual encouragement, and reassurance that you are on the right path.

What This Book Covers and How to Use It

This book has been carefully structured to provide a clear, step-by-step guide to Islam, helping you build a strong foundation in your new faith. It covers everything from the core beliefs and practices of Islam to practical aspects of daily Muslim life. You do not need to read it all at once—take your time, focus on what feels most relevant, and gradually incorporate what you learn into your life.

Each chapter is designed to provide essential knowledge in an easy-to-understand manner. In **Part 1**, you will learn about the basic tenets of Islam, including belief in Allah, the prophets, the Quran, and the fundamentals of Islamic faith. **Part 2** will introduce you to the daily practices of a Muslim, including how to pray, fast, and live according to Islamic principles. **Part 3** will guide you through the emotional and spiritual aspects of Islam, helping you strengthen your faith and overcome common struggles. **Part 4** discusses how to navigate relationships, marriage, and life as a Muslim in different social settings. Finally, **Part 5** will provide you with resources and recommendations for continuous learning and growth.

This book is not just a guide—it is your companion on this journey. If you ever feel lost or uncertain, return to these pages for reassurance and guidance. Remember, you are not alone. There are many people willing to help you, whether online, at a local masjid, or through Islamic organizations dedicated to supporting new Muslims.

Islam is a lifelong journey of learning and spiritual growth. Approach it with an open heart, and take each step at your own pace. The Prophet Muhammad

🕌 reminded us:

> **"The most beloved deeds to Allah are those that are consistent,**
> **even if they are small." (Sahih al-Bukhari)**

No matter how little you feel you know, every step you take brings you closer to Allah. Stay patient, stay committed, and embrace this journey with confidence and peace.

The Beauty of Islam – A Religion of Mercy and Guidance

Islam is not just a religion; it is a complete way of life that brings peace, purpose, and fulfillment to those who follow it. At its core, Islam is built on **mercy, compassion, and justice**. Allah describes Himself as **Ar-Rahman (The Most Merciful) and Ar-Raheem (The Especially Merciful)**, emphasizing that His love and guidance are always available to those who seek Him.

One of the most beautiful aspects of Islam is its emphasis on a **direct relationship with Allah**. Unlike other faiths where intermediaries may be required, Islam teaches that every person can speak directly to their Creator through prayer and supplication. There are no barriers between you and Allah. He hears every whisper of your heart, forgives every sincere repentance, and rewards every good deed—even the smallest ones.

Islam is also a faith of **balance and wisdom**. It encourages us to care for our bodies, minds, and souls. It teaches kindness towards parents, spouses, children, neighbors, and even strangers. It promotes justice and fairness in society, ensuring that no one is oppressed. The Quran commands:

> **"Indeed, Allah commands justice, good conduct, and giving to**
> **relatives and forbids immorality, bad conduct, and oppression."**
> **(Surah An-Nahl 16:90)**

The example of Prophet Muhammad 🕌 further demonstrates the mercy of Islam. He was known for his patience, generosity, and forgiveness. Even when people insulted or harmed him, he responded with kindness. When a man once asked him for the best advice, the Prophet ﷺ simply said:

"Do not be angry." (Sahih al-Bukhari)

Islam also provides a **clear and structured way of life**, guiding us in every aspect—from worship and family life to personal development and community service. By following its teachings, you will find a sense of inner peace and contentment that is unmatched.

As you embark on this journey, remember that Islam is not a burden—it is a gift. It is a path that leads to happiness in this life and eternal success in the Hereafter. Embrace it with an open heart, seek knowledge, and trust in the wisdom of Allah. You will soon realize that Islam is more than just a religion; it is the key to a fulfilling, meaningful, and spiritually rich life.

Part 1:
The Foundations of Islam

Chapter 1:

Understanding Tawheed
(The Oneness of God)

1. What is Tawheed?

Tawheed is the foundational concept in Islam, representing the absolute oneness and uniqueness of Allah (God). It is the core of Islamic belief and the essence of a Muslim's faith. Tawheed comes from the Arabic root word "wahhada," which means to make something one or to unify. In Islamic theology, it signifies the belief that Allah is the sole Creator, Sustainer, and Master of the universe, with no partners, equals, or rivals. This concept rejects any form of polytheism, idolatry, or association of partners with Allah. Tawheed is not merely a theoretical idea but a comprehensive framework that influences a Muslim's worship, behavior, and worldview. It emphasizes that Allah alone is worthy of worship, and all acts of devotion, such as prayer, supplication, and sacrifice, must be directed exclusively to Him. Understanding and implementing Tawheed is essential for a Muslim's spiritual and moral life, as it shapes their relationship with Allah, their purpose in life, and their accountability in the Hereafter.

2. The Three Categories of Tawheed

Tawheed is divided into three main categories, each addressing a specific aspect of Allah's oneness. These categories help Muslims understand the depth and breadth of Tawheed and ensure that their belief and actions align with Islamic teachings.

1. **Tawheed al-Rububiyyah (Oneness of Lordship):** This category affirms that Allah is the sole Creator, Provider, and Sustainer of the universe. It acknowledges that everything in existence depends on Allah for its creation, maintenance, and ultimate destiny. No one else has the power to control life, death, or the natural order. While some people may recognize Allah's role as the Creator, true Tawheed al-Rububiyyah requires complete submission to His will and rejection of any belief in other deities or forces controlling the universe.

2. **Tawheed al-Uluhiyyah (Oneness of Worship):** This aspect of Tawheed emphasizes that Allah alone is worthy of worship. It requires Muslims to direct all acts of devotion, such as prayer, fasting, charity, and supplication, exclusively to Allah. This category rejects any form of idolatry, whether it involves worshipping idols, saints, or material possessions. Tawheed al-Uluhiyyah is the most critical category, as it distinguishes true monotheism from polytheism and ensures that a person's faith is sincere and pure.

3. **Tawheed al-Asma' wa al-Sifat (Oneness of Allah's Names and Attributes):** This category focuses on the uniqueness of Allah's names and attributes as described in the Quran and Sunnah (teachings of the Prophet Muhammad). It affirms that Allah's names and attributes are perfect and unparalleled, and no creation shares or resembles them. For example, Allah is described as Ar-Rahman (the Most Merciful) and Al-Qadir (the All-Powerful), but His mercy and power are beyond human comprehension. Muslims must believe in these attributes without distorting, denying, or comparing them to those of His creation.

These three categories of Tawheed are interconnected and form the basis of Islamic monotheism. They guide Muslims in understanding Allah's greatness and their role as His servants.

3. Shirk (Associating Partners with Allah) and Its Dangers

Shirk is the gravest sin in Islam and the direct opposite of Tawheed. It refers to associating partners with Allah in any aspect of His divinity, lordship, or worship. Shirk can take many forms, including worshipping idols, attributing divine qualities to humans or objects, or believing that other beings have control over the universe. It can be major (clear and intentional) or minor (subtle and unintentional), but both are severely condemned in Islam. Major shirk, such as worshipping false gods, leads to eternal damnation if not repented from, while minor shirk, such as showing off in acts of worship, diminishes the purity of faith.

The dangers of shirk are immense. It corrupts a person's faith, nullifies good deeds, and distances them from Allah's mercy. The Quran repeatedly warns against shirk, stating that Allah will not forgive those who die in a state of shirk unless they sincerely repent. Shirk also undermines the purpose of creation, which is to worship Allah alone. By associating partners with Allah, a person commits the ultimate injustice and ingratitude, rejecting the blessings and guidance provided by their Creator.

To avoid shirk, Muslims must constantly purify their intentions, seek knowledge about Tawheed, and guard against subtle forms of shirk, such as arrogance, excessive love for worldly possessions, or relying on others instead of Allah. Understanding the dangers of shirk reinforces the importance of Tawheed and motivates Muslims to uphold the purity of their faith.

In conclusion, Tawheed is the cornerstone of Islamic belief, encompassing the oneness of Allah in His lordship, worship, and attributes. The three categories of Tawheed provide a comprehensive framework for understanding and practicing monotheism, while shirk represents the greatest threat to this belief. By adhering to Tawheed and avoiding shirk, Muslims fulfill their purpose in life and secure their success in the Hereafter.

Chapter 2:

The Six Articles of Faith

1. Belief in Allah

Belief in Allah is the cornerstone of Islamic faith, encapsulated in the concept of *Tawheed* (Oneness of Allah). Muslims believe that Allah is the sole Creator, Sustainer, and Sovereign of the universe, as stated in the Quran:

> **"Say, 'He is Allah, [who is] One, Allah, the Eternal Refuge. He neither begets nor is born, nor is there to Him any equivalent'"**
> *(Quran 112:1-4)*

This belief requires acknowledging Allah's unique attributes, such as His omnipotence, mercy, and wisdom. The Prophet Muhammad ﷺ emphasized the importance of this belief in a hadith:

> **"The most virtuous deed is to believe in Allah and His Messenger"**
> *(Sahih Bukhari)*

Belief in Allah also entails worshiping Him alone, without associating partners, as warned in the Quran:

> **"Indeed, Allah does not forgive association with Him, but He forgives what is less than that for whom He wills"** *(Quran 4:48)*

This belief shapes a Muslim's worldview, guiding their actions, morals, and purpose in life.

2. Belief in Angels

Belief in angels is a fundamental aspect of Islamic faith, as they are Allah's obedient servants created from light. They carry out His commands and play specific roles in the universe and human life. The Quran mentions angels in numerous verses, such as:

"Whoever is an enemy to Allah and His angels and His messengers and Gabriel and Michael – then indeed, Allah is an enemy to the disbelievers" *(Quran 2:98)*

Angels like Jibreel (Gabriel) delivered revelations to the prophets, while others, like Mika'il (Michael), are responsible for natural phenomena. The Prophet Muhammad ﷺ also spoke about angels, stating:

"Angels were created from light, jinn were created from smokeless fire, and Adam was created from what has been described to you" *(Sahih Muslim)*

Belief in angels reinforces the idea of an unseen world and Allah's omnipresence, as angels record human deeds, as mentioned in the Quran:

"Man does not utter any word except that with him is an observer prepared [to record]" *(Quran 50:18).*

3. Belief in the Books of Allah

Muslims believe that Allah revealed divine books to guide humanity, including the Quran, the Torah, the Psalms, and the Gospel. The Quran is the final and most complete revelation, as stated:

"Indeed, it is We who sent down the Quran and indeed, We will be its guardian" *(Quran 15:9)*

These books contain Allah's guidance and laws, tailored to the needs of their respective communities. The Prophet Muhammad ﷺ affirmed the importance of these scriptures, saying:

"If Moses were alive, he would have no choice but to follow me" *(Sunan Ibn Majah)*

highlighting the continuity and culmination of divine messages in Islam. Belief in the books of Allah underscores the importance of seeking knowledge and adhering to divine guidance.

4. Belief in the Prophets

Belief in the prophets is central to Islam, as they were chosen by Allah to convey His message to humanity. The Quran mentions numerous prophets, including Adam, Noah, Abraham, Moses, Jesus, and Muhammad (peace be upon them all):

"And We certainly sent into every nation a messenger, [saying], 'Worship Allah and avoid false gods'" *(Quran 16:36)*

Prophet Muhammad ﷺ is the final messenger, as the Quran states:

"Muhammad is not the father of any of your men, but he is the Messenger of Allah and the last of the prophets" *(Quran 33:40)*

The Prophet Muhammad ﷺ said:

"The example of me and the prophets before me is like a man who built a house, perfected it, and left only one brick missing. I am

that brick, and I am the seal of the prophets" *(Sahih Bukhari)*

Belief in the prophets inspires Muslims to follow their teachings and strive for righteousness.

5. Belief in the Day of Judgment

Belief in the Day of Judgment is a core Islamic belief, as it emphasizes accountability for one's actions. The Quran vividly describes this day:

> "And the earth will shine with the light of its Lord, and the record [of deeds] will be placed, and the prophets and the witnesses will be brought, and it will be judged between them in truth, and they will not be wronged" *(Quran 39:69)*

The Prophet Muhammad ﷺ warned about the severity of this day, saying:

> "A person's feet will not move on the Day of Judgment until they are asked about their life, how they spent it; their knowledge, how they utilized it; their wealth, how they earned and spent it; and their body, how they used it" *(Sunan At-Tirmidhi)*

This belief motivates Muslims to live purposefully, striving for good deeds and avoiding sin.

6. Belief in Qadar (Divine Decree)

Belief in Qadar, or Divine Decree, means accepting that everything happens according to Allah's will and wisdom. The Quran states:

> "No disaster strikes upon the earth or among yourselves except that it is in a register before We bring it into being – indeed that, for Allah, is easy" *(Quran 57:22)*.

The Prophet Muhammad ﷺ explained this belief, saying:

> **"Everything is by decree—even incapacity and ability"** *(Sahih Muslim)*.

This belief instills patience and trust in Allah during trials, as Muslims understand that hardships are part of a greater plan. It also encourages gratitude for blessings, recognizing them as gifts from Allah. Belief in Qadar balances human effort with divine will, fostering humility and reliance on Allah.

Chapter 3:

The Five Pillars of Islam

1. Profession of Faith (Shahada)

The Shahada, or the Islamic declaration of faith, is the cornerstone of a Muslim's belief and practice. It is articulated as *"La ilaha illallah, Muhammadur Rasulullah"* (There is no god but Allah, and Muhammad is His Messenger).

   This statement affirms the oneness of Allah (Tawhid) and the prophethood of Muhammad ﷺ. The Quran emphasizes this in Surah Al-Ikhlas (112:1-4), which declares Allah's absolute unity and uniqueness. A hadith narrated by Abu Huraira (Sahih Bukhari) states that the Prophet Muhammad ﷺ said,

> **"Faith has over seventy branches, the highest of which is the declaration of 'La ilaha illallah.'"**

Scholars like Ibn Taymiyyah explain that the Shahada is not merely a verbal affirmation but requires sincere belief, submission, and adherence to its implications in one's life. It is the first pillar of Islam and serves as the foundation for all other acts of worship.

2. Prayer (Salat)

Prayer, or Salat, is the second pillar of Islam and a direct link between the believer and Allah. It is performed five times a day, as prescribed in Surah Al-Baqarah (2:238):

"Guard your prayers, especially the middle prayer, and stand before Allah in devotion."

The Prophet Muhammad ﷺ emphasized its importance in a hadith narrated by Abdullah ibn Umar (Sahih Muslim):

"Islam is built on five [pillars]: the testimony that there is no god but Allah and that Muhammad is His Messenger, establishing prayer, paying zakat, fasting in Ramadan, and performing Hajj."

Scholars like Imam Al-Ghazali highlight that Salat is not just a physical act but a spiritual journey that purifies the heart and strengthens one's connection with Allah. It includes recitations from the Quran, physical postures like bowing (ruku) and prostration (sujood), and moments of deep reflection and humility.

3. Alms (Zakat)

Zakat, the obligatory act of giving a portion of one's wealth to those in need, is the third pillar of Islam. It is mentioned in the Quran in Surah At-Tawbah (9:60):

"Zakat is only for the poor, the needy, those employed to collect it, those whose hearts are to be reconciled, for freeing captives, for those in debt, for the cause of Allah, and for the traveler."

The Prophet Muhammad ﷺ said in a hadith narrated by Abu Huraira (Sahih Bukhari):

"Whoever pays the zakat on his wealth will have its evil removed from him."

Scholars like Ibn Qudamah explain that Zakat is not merely a charitable act but a form of worship that purifies wealth and fosters social justice. It is calculated as 2.5% of one's savings and assets, and its distribution is carefully regulated to ensure it reaches the deserving.

4. Fasting (Sawm)

Fasting during the month of Ramadan is the fourth pillar of Islam and a profound act of worship. The Quran states in Surah Al-Baqarah (2:183):

> **"O you who have believed, fasting is prescribed for you as it was prescribed for those before you, that you may become righteous."**

The Prophet Muhammad ﷺ said in a hadith narrated by Abu Huraira (Sahih Bukhari):

> **"Whoever fasts during Ramadan out of faith and seeking reward, his previous sins will be forgiven."**

Scholars like Imam An-Nawawi emphasize that fasting is not just abstaining from food and drink but also from sinful behavior, as it cultivates self-discipline, empathy for the poor, and spiritual growth. The night prayers (Taraweeh) and increased recitation of the Quran during Ramadan further enhance its significance.

5. Pilgrimage (Hajj)

Hajj, the pilgrimage to Mecca, is the fifth pillar of Islam and a once-in-a-lifetime obligation for those who are physically and financially able. The Quran mentions in Surah Al-Imran (3:97):

> **"And Hajj to the House is a duty that mankind owes to Allah, for those who are able to undertake it."**

The Prophet Muhammad ﷺ said in a hadith narrated by Abu Huraira (Sahih Bukhari):

"Whoever performs Hajj for Allah's sake and does not have sexual relations nor commits sin, will return as sinless as a newborn baby."

Scholars like Ibn Kathir explain that Hajj symbolizes the unity of Muslims, as millions gather from diverse backgrounds to worship Allah. The rituals, such as Tawaf (circumambulation of the Kaaba) and standing at Arafat, commemorate the legacy of Prophet Ibrahim (Abraham) and his family, reinforcing themes of sacrifice, devotion, and submission to Allah.

Chapter 4:

The Quran
The Final Revelatio

1. What is the Quran?

The Quran is the holy book of Islam, believed by Muslims to be the literal word of God (Allah) as revealed to the Prophet Muhammad ﷺ through the Angel Gabriel over a period of 23 years. It is the ultimate source of guidance for Muslims, addressing matters of faith, morality, law, and spirituality. The Quran is written in classical Arabic and is divided into 114 chapters (Surahs), which vary in length. Each Surah is composed of verses (Ayahs), totaling 6,236 verses. The Quran emphasizes its divine origin, stating:

> **"Indeed, it is We who sent down the Qur'an and indeed, We will be its guardian." (Quran 15:9)**

This verse highlights the belief that the Quran has been preserved without alteration since its revelation. Scholars like Ibn Kathir explain that the Quran's miraculous nature lies in its linguistic excellence, scientific accuracy, and timeless relevance. It serves as a comprehensive guide for humanity, offering solutions to personal, social, and spiritual challenges.

2. Why is the Quran Special?

The Quran holds a unique position in Islam and among religious texts due to its unparalleled linguistic beauty, divine origin, and profound impact on individuals and societies. Its eloquence and depth have been acknowledged even by non–Muslim scholars. The Quran challenges humanity to produce a single chapter like it:

> **"And if you are in doubt about what We have sent down upon Our Servant [Muhammad], then produce a Surah the like thereof and call upon your witnesses other than Allah, if you should be truthful."**
> **(Quran 2:23)**

This challenge remains unmet, underscoring the Quran's miraculous nature. Additionally, the Quran is special because it is a living text, recited daily by millions worldwide. It provides comfort, guidance, and inspiration. The Prophet Muhammad ﷺ said:

> **"The best among you are those who learn the Quran and teach it."**
> **(Sahih al-Bukhari)**

Scholars like Imam Al-Ghazali emphasize that the Quran's teachings transform hearts and minds, fostering a deep connection between the Creator and His creation. Its preservation, both in written form and through memorization, further distinguishes it as a unique and enduring miracle.

3. How to Read and Understand the Quran

Reading and understanding the Quran requires both spiritual intention and intellectual effort. Muslims are encouraged to approach the Quran with purity, humility, and a sincere desire to seek guidance. Before reading, it is recommended to perform ablution (Wudu) and seek refuge from Satan:

"So when you recite the Qur'an, seek refuge in Allah from Satan, the expelled [from His mercy]." (Quran 16:98)

Understanding the Quran involves studying its language, context, and interpretations (Tafsir). Scholars like Ibn Taymiyyah emphasize the importance of learning Arabic to grasp the Quran's nuances fully. However, translations and commentaries are valuable tools for non-Arabic speakers. The Prophet Muhammad ﷺ said:

"Whoever recites a letter from the Book of Allah will be credited with a good deed, and a good deed gets a ten-fold reward. I do not say that Alif-Lam-Mim is one letter, but Alif is a letter, Lam is a letter, and Mim is a letter." (Sunan at-Tirmidhi)

This Hadith highlights the spiritual reward of reciting the Quran, even if one does not fully understand it. To deepen comprehension, one should study Tafsir works by renowned scholars like Ibn Kathir, Al-Tabari, or Al-Qurtubi, which provide historical context and explanations of verses. Additionally, reflecting (Tadabbur) on the Quran's message is essential:

"Then do they not reflect upon the Qur'an, or are there locks upon [their] hearts?" (Quran 47:24)

By combining recitation, reflection, and study, one can unlock the Quran's profound wisdom and apply its teachings to daily life.

Chapter 5:

The Sunnah and Hadith
The Example of the Prophet ﷺ

1. Who is Prophet Muhammadﷺ?

Prophet Muhammad ﷺ is the final messenger of Allah, sent as a mercy to all of creation. He was born in Mecca in 570 CE, a descendant of the noble lineage of Prophet Ibrahim (Abraham) through his son Ismail (Ishmael). At the age of 40, while meditating in the cave of Hira, he received the first revelation from Allah through the Angel Jibril (Gabriel). This marked the beginning of his prophethood, which lasted 23 years. His mission was to guide humanity to the worship of One God (Tawhid) and to establish justice, compassion, and morality in a world plagued by ignorance (Jahiliyyah). The Quran describes him as the **"seal of the prophets" (Quran 33:40)**, meaning no prophet will come after him. Allah says in the Quran:

> **"We have sent you (O Muhammad) not but as a mercy for the worlds." (Quran 21:107)**

The Prophet ﷺ exemplified the highest moral character, as described by his wife Aisha (may Allah be pleased with her): **"His character was the Quran." (Muslim)** He endured immense hardships, including persecution, exile, and loss, to deliver the message of Islam. His life serves as the perfect example for humanity, encompassing every aspect of life, from worship to social conduct.

Scholars like Ibn Kathir emphasize that his 🕌 teachings and actions provide a comprehensive guide for all aspects of life. For instance, his patience during the boycott of the Banu Hashim clan and his forgiveness after the conquest of Mecca demonstrate his unparalleled character.

2. Understanding Hadith Literature

Hadith literature comprises the sayings, actions, and approvals of Prophet Muhammad 🕌, meticulously recorded by his companions and later scholars. It serves as the second primary source of Islamic guidance after the Quran. The science of Hadith involves rigorous methods to verify the authenticity of each narration, including examining the chain of narrators (isnad) and the text (matn). This meticulous process ensures that only authentic narrations are preserved. The Quran emphasizes the importance of following the Prophet's teachings:

> **"And whatever the Messenger has given you, take it; and what he has forbidden you, refrain from it." (Quran 59:7)**

One of the most famous Hadith collections is Sahih al-Bukhari, which contains over 7,000 authentic narrations. Imam Bukhari spent 16 years compiling this work, ensuring each Hadith met strict criteria. Another renowned collection is Sahih Muslim, which is equally respected for its authenticity. Scholars like Imam Nawawi highlight that Hadith literature is essential for understanding the Quran and implementing its teachings in daily life. For example, the Prophet 🕌 said:

> **"Whoever obeys me has obeyed Allah, and whoever disobeys me has disobeyed Allah." (Bukhari)**

This underscores the inseparable link between the Quran and the Sunnah. Hadith literature also provides context for Quranic verses, such as the details of Salah (prayer), Zakat (charity), and Hajj (pilgrimage), which are not fully explained in the Quran alone.

3. The Importance of Following the Sunnah

The Sunnah refers to the practices and traditions of Prophet Muhammad ﷺ, which provide a practical framework for implementing Islamic teachings. Following the Sunnah is not only an act of worship but also a means of attaining Allah's love and guidance. The Quran states:

> "Indeed, in the Messenger of Allah you have an excellent example for whoever has hope in Allah and the Last Day and remembers Allah often." (Quran 33:21)

The Prophet ﷺ emphasized the importance of adhering to his Sunnah, warning against innovations (bid'ah) in religion. He said:

> "Whoever introduces something new into this matter of ours (Islam) that is not part of it will have it rejected." (Bukhari and Muslim)

Scholars like Imam Malik and Imam Shafi'i have stressed that the Sunnah is a divine source of guidance, complementing the Quran. For instance, the details of how to perform Salah (prayer) are derived from the Sunnah, as the Quran provides general commands but not specific instructions. The Prophet ﷺ said:

> "Pray as you have seen me praying." (Bukhari)

By following the Sunnah, Muslims align themselves with the Prophet's ﷺ way of life, ensuring their actions are in harmony with divine will. The Sunnah also addresses various aspects of life, including family relations, business ethics, and social justice. For example, the Prophet ﷺ encouraged kindness to neighbors, saying:

"Jibril kept recommending treating neighbors with kindness until I thought he would assign a share of inheritance." (Bukhari and Muslim)

In conclusion, Prophet Muhammad ﷺ is the ultimate role model for humanity, and his teachings, preserved in the Hadith and Sunnah, provide a comprehensive guide for living a righteous life. By adhering to these sources, Muslims fulfill their duty to Allah and follow the path of the Prophet ﷺ, ensuring success in this life and the Hereafter. The Quran, Hadith, and Sunnah together form a complete system of guidance, enabling Muslims to navigate the challenges of life while remaining steadfast in their faith. As scholars like Ibn Taymiyyah have noted, the Sunnah is the practical manifestation of the Quran, and following it is a means of drawing closer to Allah and attaining His pleasure.

Part 2:
Daily Life as a Muslim

Chapter 6:

How to Perform Wudu
(Ablution) and Salah (Prayer)

1. Step-by-Step Guide to Wudu

Wudu, or ablution, is a fundamental act of purification in Islam, essential for performing Salah and other acts of worship. The process is outlined in the Quran and Sunnah, ensuring Muslims follow a precise method. Allah says in the Quran:

> **"O you who have believed, when you rise to [perform] prayer, wash your faces and your forearms to the elbows and wipe over your heads and wash your feet to the ankles." (Quran 5:6)**

This verse provides the foundational steps for Wudu. The Prophet Muhammad ﷺ further elaborated on the process in numerous hadiths. For instance, in Sahih al-Bukhari, it is narrated that the Prophet said:

> **"Whoever performs Wudu like this Wudu of mine and then offers two Rak'at of Salah without letting his thoughts wander, his past sins will be forgiven."**

Scholars like Imam Nawawi emphasize the importance of intention (niyyah) before starting Wudu, as it transforms the act into an act of worship. The steps include washing the hands, rinsing the mouth, sniffing water into the nose, washing the face, arms, wiping the head, and washing the feet, ensuring no part is left dry.

2. How to Perform Salah

Salah, the second pillar of Islam, is a direct connection between the believer and Allah. The Quran repeatedly emphasizes its importance:

> **"Establish prayer, for prayer restrains from shameful and unjust deeds." (Quran 29:45)**

The Prophet Muhammad ﷺ demonstrated the method of Salah in detail. In a hadith narrated by Abu Hurairah, the Prophet said:

> **"Pray as you have seen me praying." (Sahih al-Bukhari)**

This instruction underscores the necessity of following the Prophet's example. Salah begins with the Takbir (saying "Allahu Akbar"), followed by recitation of Surah Al-Fatihah and additional verses, bowing (Ruku), prostration (Sujood), and concluding with the Tashahhud and Tasleem. Scholars like Ibn Qayyim highlight the spiritual and physical discipline Salah instills, urging Muslims to perform it with humility (khushu) and focus.

3. Common Mistakes in Prayer

Despite its significance, many Muslims unintentionally make errors during Salah. The Prophet ﷺ warned against such mistakes, saying:

> **"How many people pray but gain nothing from their prayer except fatigue." (Sunan Ibn Majah)**

Common errors include rushing through Salah, failing to achieve proper concentration, and incorrect physical postures. For example, some neglect the proper alignment of the back during Ruku or fail to place the forehead firmly on the ground during Sujood. The Quran reminds us:

"Successful indeed are the believers, those who offer their Salah with all solemnity and full submissiveness." (Quran 23:1-2)

Scholars like Imam Ghazali stress the importance of understanding the meanings of the recited verses and supplications to enhance focus. Additionally, failing to perform Wudu correctly or praying in unclean clothing can invalidate Salah. By addressing these mistakes, Muslims can ensure their prayers are accepted and spiritually rewarding.

Each of these topics underscores the importance of adhering to the Quranic guidelines and the Prophet's teachings, as explained by Islamic scholars, to perfect acts of worship and draw closer to Allah.

Chapter 7:

Fasting in Ramadan
Meaning and Practice

1. The Spiritual Purpose of Fasting

Fasting, particularly during the month of Ramadan, holds profound spiritual significance in Islam. It is not merely an act of abstaining from food and drink but a means of attaining taqwa (God-consciousness) and purifying the soul. Allah says in the Quran:

> **"O you who have believed, decreed upon you is fasting as it was decreed upon those before you that you may become righteous."**
> **(Quran 2:183)**

This verse highlights that fasting is a divine commandment aimed at cultivating self-discipline, empathy for the less fortunate, and a deeper connection with Allah. The Prophet Muhammad ﷺ emphasized the spiritual rewards of fasting, stating:

> **"Every deed of the son of Adam is for himself except fasting; it is for Me, and I shall reward it." (Sahih al-Bukhari)**

Scholars like Ibn Qayyim al-Jawziyya explain that fasting weakens the physical desires and strengthens the soul, allowing the believer to focus on worship and self-reflection. It is a time to seek forgiveness, increase in good deeds, and draw closer to Allah through prayer, Quran recitation, and acts of charity.

2. Rules and Regulations of Fasting

The rules of fasting in Islam are derived from the Quran, the Sunnah of the Prophet ﷺ, and the consensus of scholars. Fasting during Ramadan is obligatory for every adult Muslim who is physically and mentally capable. Allah says:

> "The month of Ramadan [is that] in which was revealed the Quran, a guidance for the people and clear proofs of guidance and criterion. So whoever sights [the new moon of] the month, let him fast it." (Quran 2:185)

The fast begins at dawn (Fajr) and ends at sunset (Maghrib). During this time, Muslims must abstain from food, drink, and marital relations. The Prophet ﷺ said:

> "Whoever does not give up false speech and evil actions, Allah is not in need of his leaving his food and drink." (Sahih al-Bukhari)

This hadith underscores that fasting is not just about physical abstinence but also about avoiding sinful behavior. Scholars like Imam al-Nawawi explain that fasting is invalidated by intentional eating, drinking, or sexual activity, but unintentional actions do not break the fast. Exceptions are made for those who are ill, traveling, pregnant, breastfeeding, or menstruating, as Allah says:

> "And whoever is ill or on a journey – then an equal number of other days." (Quran 2:185)

3. Common Questions About Fasting

Many Muslims have questions about the specifics of fasting, and these are often addressed through the Quran, hadith, and scholarly explanations. For example, a common question is whether brushing teeth or using mouthwash invalidates the fast. Scholars like Ibn Taymiyyah state that these actions are permissible as long as nothing is swallowed. The Prophet ﷺ said:

> "If you forget [that you are fasting] and eat or drink, then complete your fast, for Allah has fed you and given you to drink." (Sahih Muslim)

Another frequent question is about the ruling on swallowing saliva. Scholars agree that swallowing saliva does not break the fast, as it is a natural bodily function. However, intentionally swallowing food, drink, or other substances does invalidate the fast. Additionally, questions about the timing of Suhoor (pre-dawn meal) and Iftar (breaking the fast) are clarified by the Prophet's ﷺ guidance:

> "Take Suhoor, for in Suhoor there is blessing." (Sahih al-Bukhari)

And:

> "The people will continue to prosper as long as they hasten to break the fast." (Sahih al-Bukhari)

These teachings emphasize the importance of adhering to the prescribed times and seeking the blessings associated with them. Scholars also address modern issues, such as the use of medical injections or eye drops, ruling that they do not break the fast unless they provide nourishment.

In conclusion, fasting in Islam is a multifaceted act of worship with deep spiritual, physical, and social dimensions. It is governed by clear rules and regulations, and common questions are addressed through the guidance of the Quran, the Sunnah, and the interpretations of scholars. By adhering to these principles, Muslims can fulfill this pillar of Islam in a manner that is pleasing to Allah and beneficial to their spiritual growth.

Chapter 8:

Zakat and Charity
The Spirit of Giving

1. Who Must Pay Zakat?

Zakat is one of the five pillars of Islam and is obligatory for every Muslim who meets specific criteria. According to Islamic teachings, Zakat is mandatory for those who possess wealth equal to or exceeding the Nisab (a minimum threshold) and have held it for a full lunar year. The Quran explicitly states:

> "Take, [O, Muhammad], from their wealth a charity by which you purify them and cause them to increase, and invoke [Allah's blessings] upon them. Indeed, your invocations are reassurance for them. And Allah is Hearing and Knowing."
> (Quran 9:103)

This verse highlights the purification aspect of Zakat, which cleanses one's wealth and soul. Scholars like Imam Ibn Kathir explain that Zakat is a means of redistributing wealth in society, ensuring that the needy are supported. The Prophet Muhammad 🙵 also emphasized its importance, saying:

> "Islam is built on five [pillars]: the testimony that there is no deity worthy of worship except Allah and that Muhammad is the Messenger of Allah, establishing prayer, paying Zakat, fasting

Ramadan, and performing Hajj if one is able." (Sahih al-Bukhari)

Thus, Zakat is a divine obligation for those who meet the conditions, and neglecting it is considered a major sin.

2. Types of Charity in Islam

Charity in Islam is not limited to Zakat; it encompasses various forms of giving, each with its own significance. The Quran and Hadith mention multiple types of charity, including Sadaqah (voluntary charity), Sadaqah Jariyah (ongoing charity), and Zakat al-Fitr (charity given at the end of Ramadan). The Quran says:

> **"The example of those who spend their wealth in the way of Allah is like a seed [of grain] that grows seven spikes; in each spike is a hundred grains. And Allah multiplies [His reward] for whom He wills. And Allah is all-Encompassing and Knowing." (Quran 2:261)**

This verse illustrates the immense reward for spending in the path of Allah. The Prophet Muhammad ﷺ further elaborated on the types of charity, stating:

> **"Every act of kindness is Sadaqah." (Sahih Muslim)**

Scholars like Imam Al-Ghazali emphasize that charity is not limited to monetary donations; even a smile or a good deed can be considered Sadaqah. Sadaqah Jariyah, such as building a well or funding education, continues to benefit the giver even after death. The Prophet said:

> **"When a person dies, their deeds come to an end except for three: ongoing charity, beneficial knowledge, or a righteous child who prays for them." (Sahih Muslim)**

Thus, Islam encourages a wide range of charitable acts, each with its own unique rewards.

3. The Rewards of Giving

The act of giving in Islam is highly rewarded, both in this world and the hereafter. The Quran and Hadith are replete with promises of immense blessings for those who give generously. Allah says:

> **"Whoever does righteousness, whether male or female, while being a believer – We will surely cause them to live a good life, and We will surely give them their reward [in the Hereafter] according to the best of what they used to do." (Quran 16:97)**

This verse assures believers that their charitable deeds will not go unnoticed. The Prophet Muhammad ﷺ also highlighted the spiritual and worldly benefits of giving, stating:

> **"Charity does not decrease wealth." (Sahih Muslim)**

Scholars like Imam Ibn Taymiyyah explain that giving charity purifies the heart, increases blessings in one's wealth, and protects against calamities. The Prophet further said:

> **"The believer's shade on the Day of Resurrection will be their charity." (Al-Tirmidhi)**

This Hadith underscores the protective nature of charity in the afterlife. Additionally, the Quran promises:

> **"Indeed, the men who practice charity and the women who practice charity and [they who] have loaned Allah a goodly loan – it will be multiplied for them, and they will have a noble reward."**

(Quran 57:18)

Thus, the rewards of giving are multifaceted, encompassing spiritual growth, worldly blessings, and eternal salvation.

Chapter 9:

Halal and Haram
What is Permissible?

1. Halal Food and Drinks

In Islam, the concept of halal (permissible) food and drinks is central to a Muslim's daily life. Halal refers to what is lawful and wholesome according to Islamic law (Shariah). The Quran explicitly outlines the principles of halal consumption, emphasizing the importance of eating pure and permissible sustenance. Allah says in the Quran:

> "O mankind, eat from whatever is on earth [that is] lawful and good and do not follow the footsteps of Satan. Indeed, he is to you a clear enemy." (Quran 2:168)

This verse highlights the importance of consuming what is lawful (halal) and good (tayyib). Halal food includes meat from animals slaughtered in the name of Allah, with specific guidelines to ensure humane treatment and proper drainage of blood. The Prophet Muhammad ﷺ also emphasized the significance of halal consumption, stating:

> "O people, Allah is Pure, and He only accepts what is pure. Indeed, Allah has commanded the believers as He has commanded His Messengers, saying, 'O Messengers, eat from the good foods and

work righteousness.'" **(Sahih Muslim)**

Scholars like Ibn Kathir explain that halal food not only fulfills physical needs but also purifies the soul, as consuming unlawful (haram) food distances a person from Allah's blessings. Thus, halal food is a means of maintaining spiritual and physical well-being.

2. The Prohibition of Alcohol and Pork

Islam strictly prohibits the consumption of alcohol and pork, as they are considered impure and harmful to both the body and soul. The Quran explicitly forbids these substances, stating:

> **"O you who have believed, indeed, intoxicants, gambling, [sacrificing on] stone alters [to other than Allah], and divining arrows are but defilement from the work of Satan, so avoid it that you may be successful." (Quran 5:90)**

Alcohol is prohibited due to its intoxicating effects, which impair judgment and lead to sinful behavior. Similarly, pork is forbidden as it is considered inherently impure. The Prophet Muhammad ﷺ reinforced this prohibition, saying:

> **"Allah has forbidden the consumption of alcohol, and whoever drinks it and does not repent, it will not be accepted from him on the Day of Judgment." (Sahih Bukhari)**

Scholars like Imam Al-Ghazali explain that these prohibitions are not arbitrary but are based on divine wisdom. Alcohol and pork are harmful to health, and their prohibition aligns with Islam's emphasis on preserving life and purity. By abstaining from these substances, Muslims demonstrate obedience to Allah and protect their physical and spiritual well-being.

3. The Concept of Purity in Islam

Purity (taharah) is a fundamental concept in Islam, encompassing both physical and spiritual cleanliness. The Quran and Hadith emphasize the importance of purity in worship and daily life. Allah says:

> **"Indeed, Allah loves those who are constantly repentant and loves those who purify themselves." (Quran 2:222)**

This verse underscores the connection between purity and divine love. Physical purity is achieved through rituals like ablution (wudu) and ghusl (full body wash), which are prerequisites for acts of worship such as prayer. The Prophet Muhammad ﷺ said:

> **"Cleanliness is half of faith." (Sahih Muslim)**

Scholars like Ibn Qayyim Al-Jawziyya explain that purity is not limited to physical cleanliness but extends to moral and spiritual purity. Avoiding haram food, maintaining good hygiene, and purifying the heart from sins are all aspects of this concept. Purity is a means of drawing closer to Allah and attaining His pleasure, as it reflects a Muslim's commitment to living a life of righteousness and devotion.

By adhering to these principles, Muslims ensure that their actions align with Islamic teachings, fostering a holistic sense of purity in their lives.

Chapter 10:

Islamic Etiquette and Manners

1. Greeting Others in Islam

In Islam, greeting others is not merely a social custom but an act of worship that fosters love and unity among people. The Islamic greeting "As-Salamu Alaikum" (Peace be upon you) is deeply rooted in the Quran and Sunnah. Allah says in the Quran:

> "When you are greeted with a greeting, greet in return with what is better than it, or at least return it equally. Indeed, Allah is ever a careful Accountant of all things." (Quran 4:86)

This verse emphasizes the importance of responding to greetings with kindness. The Prophet Muhammad ﷺ also encouraged spreading greetings, as narrated in Sahih Muslim:

> "You will not enter Paradise until you believe, and you will not believe until you love one another. Shall I not tell you something which, if you do, you will love one another? Spread the greeting of peace among yourselves."

Scholars like Ibn Kathir explain that the greeting "As-Salamu Alaikum" carries a profound meaning, as it invokes peace, mercy, and blessings from Allah. It is a reminder of the Islamic values of harmony and goodwill.

2. Proper Dress Code for Men and Women

Islam places great emphasis on modesty in dress for both men and women, as it reflects piety and self-respect. Allah commands in the Quran:

> "O children of Adam, We have bestowed upon you clothing to conceal your private parts and as adornment. But the clothing of righteousness—that is best. That is from the signs of Allah that perhaps they will remember." (Quran 7:26)

For men, the Prophet Muhammad ﷺ warned against wearing clothing that is too long or extravagant, as narrated in Sahih Bukhari:

> "Whoever allows his garment to drag out of pride, Allah will not look at him on the Day of Resurrection."

For women, the Quran instructs:

> "And tell the believing women to reduce [some] of their vision and guard their private parts and not expose their adornment except that which [necessarily] appears thereof…" (Quran 24:31)

Scholars like Imam Al-Ghazali explain that modesty in dress is a means of protecting one's dignity and avoiding societal corruption. The dress code is not merely about covering the body but also about embodying humility and devotion to Allah.

3. Respecting Parents and Elders

Respecting parents and elders is a fundamental principle in Islam, as it is a reflection of gratitude and obedience to Allah. The Quran repeatedly emphasizes the importance of kindness to parents:

"And your Lord has decreed that you not worship except Him, and to parents, good treatment. Whether one or both of them reach old age [while] with you, say not to them [so much as] 'uff' [a word of disrespect] and do not repel them but speak to them a noble word." (Quran 17:23)

The Prophet Muhammad ﷺ also highlighted the significance of respecting elders, as narrated in Sahih Bukhari:

"He is not one of us who does not show mercy to our young and respect to our elders."

Scholars like Ibn Al-Qayyim explain that respecting parents is a form of worship, as it is directly linked to pleasing Allah. Elders, due to their wisdom and experience, deserve honor and kindness, as this fosters a harmonious and respectful society.

By adhering to these teachings, Muslims can cultivate a life of piety, modesty, and respect, fulfilling their duties to Allah and society.

Part 3:
Strengthening Your Faith

Chapter 11:

The Importance of Seeking Knowledge

1. The Role of Knowledge in Islam

In Islam, knowledge holds a paramount position, as it is the foundation of faith and worship. The Quran and Hadith emphasize the importance of seeking knowledge, making it an obligation for every Muslim. Allah says in the Quran:

> "Read in the name of your Lord who created—Created man from a clinging substance. Read, and your Lord is the Most Generous—Who taught by the pen—Taught man that which he knew not."
> (Quran 96:1-5)

This verse underscores the significance of learning and reflection. The Prophet Muhammad ﷺ also highlighted the value of knowledge, stating:

> "Seeking knowledge is an obligation upon every Muslim." (Sunan Ibn Majah)

Scholars like Imam Al-Ghazali explained that knowledge is the path to understanding Allah's creation and fulfilling one's purpose in life. It is not limited to religious studies but extends to all fields that benefit humanity, as long as they align with Islamic principles. Knowledge in Islam is a means of drawing closer to Allah, combating ignorance, and fostering a just and enlightened society.

2. Recommended Islamic Books and Scholars

Islamic literature is vast, and certain books and scholars have profoundly influenced the understanding of the faith. For beginners, *"The Clear Quran"* by Dr. Mustafa Khattab is an excellent translation with explanations. For Hadith, *"Riyad as-Salihin"* by Imam Nawawi is a comprehensive collection of Prophetic teachings. In theology, *"Aqeedah Tahawiyyah"* by Imam Tahawi is a cornerstone text.

Classical scholars like Imam Ibn Taymiyyah, known for his works on Islamic jurisprudence and theology, and Imam Al-Bukhari, who compiled the most authentic Hadith collection, *"Sahih al-Bukhari,"* are essential references. Contemporary scholars such as Sheikh Yusuf Qaradawi and Dr. Zakir Naik have also contributed significantly to explaining Islam in modern contexts. The Prophet ﷺ said:

"The scholars are the heirs of the prophets." (Sunan Abi Dawud)

This Hadith highlights the importance of learning from qualified scholars who preserve and transmit Islamic knowledge accurately.

3. How to Learn Islam Step by Step

Learning Islam systematically ensures a strong foundation in faith and practice. Begin with the basics of *Tawheed* (monotheism), as Allah says:

"So know that there is no deity except Allah and ask forgiveness for your sin." (Quran 47:19)

Study the five pillars of Islam: Shahadah, Salah, Zakah, Sawm, and Hajj. Use reliable resources like *"The Book of Tawheed"* by Muhammad ibn Abd al-Wahhab and *"Fiqh us-Sunnah"* by Sayyid Sabiq. Next, delve into the life of the Prophet ﷺ through *"The Sealed Nectar"* by Safiur Rahman Mubarakpuri. Consistent learning is key. The Prophet ﷺ said:

> **"Take benefit of five before five: your youth before your old age, your health before your sickness, your wealth before your poverty, your free time before you are preoccupied, and your life before your death." (Al-Hakim)**

Seek knowledge from qualified teachers, join study circles, and utilize online platforms like Islamic Online University. Balance your learning with action, as knowledge without practice is futile. By following these steps, one can develop a deep and meaningful understanding of Islam.

Chapter 12:

Building a Strong Connection with Allah

1. The Power of Du'a (Supplication)

Du'a, or supplication, is one of the most powerful acts of worship in Islam, serving as a direct connection between the believer and Allah. It is a manifestation of humility, dependence, and trust in Allah's mercy and wisdom. The Quran emphasizes the importance of du'a in numerous verses, such as:

> **"And your Lord says, 'Call upon Me; I will respond to you.' Indeed, those who disdain My worship will enter Hell [rendered] contemptible." (Quran 40:60)**

This verse highlights Allah's promise to answer those who call upon Him sincerely. Similarly, the Prophet Muhammad ﷺ said:

> **"Du'a is the essence of worship." (Tirmidhi)**

Scholars like Ibn Taymiyyah explain that du'a is not merely a request but an act of worship that strengthens one's relationship with Allah. It is a tool for seeking guidance, forgiveness, and blessings, and it reflects the believer's acknowledgment of Allah's power over all matters.

The Prophet ﷺ also said:

"Nothing can change the Divine decree except du'a." (Ibn Majah)

This hadith underscores the transformative power of supplication, as it can alter one's circumstances and bring about Allah's mercy. Scholars like Imam Al-Nawawi emphasize that du'a should be made with sincerity, humility, and certainty in Allah's response, even if the answer is delayed or comes in an unexpected form. The Quran further reassures believers:

"When My servants ask you concerning Me, indeed I am near. I respond to the invocation of the supplicant when he calls upon Me." (Quran 2:186)

This verse reminds us that Allah is always close to His servants, listening to their pleas and responding in ways that are best for them. By turning to Allah in du'a, believers can find solace, strength, and hope, knowing that their Creator is the ultimate source of all solutions.

2. How to Increase Your Iman (Faith)

Iman, or faith, is the foundation of a Muslim's life, and it fluctuates based on one's actions and connection with Allah. To increase iman, one must engage in consistent acts of worship, such as prayer, Quran recitation, and remembrance of Allah. The Quran states:

"Those who have believed and whose hearts are assured by the remembrance of Allah. Unquestionably, by the remembrance of Allah, hearts are assured." (Quran 13:28)

This verse highlights the importance of dhikr (remembrance of Allah) in strengthening one's faith and achieving tranquility. The Prophet Muhammad ﷺ also emphasized the importance of good deeds, saying:

"Faith wears out in the heart of any one of you just as clothes wear

out, so ask Allah to renew the faith in your hearts." (Al-Hakim)

This hadith illustrates that iman requires constant care and renewal, much like clothing that becomes worn over time.

Scholars like Imam Al-Ghazali explain that iman is strengthened through knowledge, reflection, and action. By studying the Quran, pondering over its meanings, and implementing its teachings, a believer can elevate their faith. For example, reflecting on verses like:

"Indeed, in the creation of the heavens and the earth and the alternation of the night and the day are signs for those of understanding(Quran 3:190)

can deepen one's appreciation of Allah's greatness and increase iman. Additionally, surrounding oneself with righteous company and avoiding sins are crucial for maintaining and increasing iman. The Prophet ﷺ said:

"A person is upon the religion of their close friend, so let one of you look at whom they befriend." (Abu Dawud)

This hadith underscores the influence of companionship on one's faith. By engaging in acts of worship, seeking knowledge, and fostering good relationships, a believer can steadily increase their iman and draw closer to Allah.

3. Finding Inner Peace in Islam

Inner peace is a state of tranquility and contentment that comes from a deep connection with Allah and adherence to His guidance. In Islam, true peace is found through submission to Allah's will and trust in His plan. The Quran states:

"Verily, in the remembrance of Allah do hearts find rest." (Quran

13:28)

This verse highlights that remembrance of Allah (dhikr) is the key to calming the soul and achieving inner peace. The Prophet Muhammad ﷺ also taught that peace comes from reliance on Allah, saying:

> **"How wonderful is the case of a believer! There is good for him in everything, and this applies only to a believer. If prosperity attends him, he expresses gratitude to Allah, and that is good for him; and if adversity befalls him, he endures it patiently, and that is good for him." (Muslim)**

This hadith illustrates that a believer's faith allows them to find peace in both good and challenging times, knowing that everything is from Allah and serves a greater purpose.

Scholars like Ibn Al-Qayyim explain that inner peace is achieved by aligning one's heart with the remembrance of Allah and trusting in His wisdom. He writes in his book *"Al-Fawa'id"* that the heart finds no rest except in the love and remembrance of Allah. Additionally, the Quran reassures believers:

> **"So remember Me; I will remember you. And be grateful to Me and do not deny Me." (Quran 2:152)**

This verse emphasizes the reciprocal relationship between Allah and His servants, where remembrance and gratitude lead to divine blessings and inner peace. By performing acts of worship, such as prayer, reading the Quran, and making du'a, believers can cultivate a sense of calm and contentment. Furthermore, avoiding sins and seeking forgiveness are essential for maintaining inner peace, as sins create a barrier between the believer and Allah. The Prophet ﷺ said:

> **"When a person commits a sin, a black spot appears on his heart. If he repents, it is removed, but if he persists, it spreads until it**

covers the entire heart." (Ibn Majah)

This hadith highlights the importance of repentance in preserving the purity of the heart and achieving inner peace. Through faith, remembrance, and righteous actions, Muslims can find true and lasting peace in this life and the hereafter.

By adhering to these principles and drawing from the Quran, hadith, and the wisdom of Islamic scholars, believers can unlock the power of du'a, strengthen their iman, and attain inner peace, ultimately leading to a fulfilling and spiritually enriched life.

Chapter 13:

Overcoming Doubts and Hardships

1. Dealing with Questions and Uncertainty

Life is filled with moments of doubt and questions that challenge our faith and understanding. Islam teaches us to approach uncertainty with trust in Allah's wisdom and to seek knowledge to strengthen our conviction. The Quran reminds us,

> "And rely upon the Ever-Living who does not die, and exalt [Allah] with His praise. And sufficient is He to be, with the sins of His servants, Acquainted." (Quran 25:58).

This verse encourages believers to place their reliance on Allah, who is eternal and all-knowing, even when answers are not immediately clear. The Prophet Muhammad ﷺ also emphasized the importance of seeking knowledge, as narrated in a hadith:

> "Whoever treads a path in search of knowledge, Allah will make easy for him a path to Paradise." (Sahih Muslim).

Scholars like Ibn Qayyim al-Jawziyya explain that uncertainty is a test of faith, and through patience and seeking guidance, one can find clarity. He writes in

"Miftah Dar al-Sa'adah" that questions and doubts are opportunities to deepen one's understanding and connection with Allah.

2. How to Handle Family and Friends' Reactions

Navigating the reactions of family and friends, especially when they differ from our beliefs or choices, can be challenging. Islam provides guidance on maintaining kindness and patience while staying firm in faith. The Quran advises,

> **"And We have enjoined upon man [care] for his parents. His mother carried him, [increasing her] in weakness upon weakness, and his weaning is in two years. Be grateful to Me and to your parents; to Me is the [final] destination." (Quran 31:14).**

This verse highlights the importance of respecting and honoring family ties, even in difficult situations. The Prophet Muhammad ﷺ demonstrated this when he faced opposition from his own tribe. He said,

> **"The best of you are those who are best to their families." (Sunan Ibn Majah).**

Scholars like Imam Ghazali emphasize the balance between maintaining relationships and upholding one's faith. In *"Ihya Ulum al-Din,"* he explains that gentle persuasion and exemplary behavior are more effective than confrontation when dealing with differing opinions.

3. Staying Patient in Difficult Times

Patience (sabr) is a cornerstone of Islamic teachings, especially during trials and hardships. The Quran repeatedly emphasizes the virtue of patience, stating,

"O you who have believed, seek help through patience and prayer. Indeed, Allah is with the patient." (Quran 2:153).

This verse reminds believers that Allah's support is always near for those who remain steadfast. The Prophet Muhammad ﷺ also exemplified patience during his life, saying,

"How wonderful is the affair of the believer, for his affairs are all good, and this applies to no one but the believer. If something good happens to him, he is thankful for it, and that is good for him. If something bad happens to him, he bears it with patience, and that is good for him." (Sahih Muslim).

Scholars like Ibn Taymiyyah explain in *"Al-Ubudiyyah"* that patience is not merely enduring hardship but actively seeking Allah's pleasure through it. He writes that trials are a means of purification and elevation in the sight of Allah, and patience transforms suffering into a source of spiritual growth.

In conclusion, dealing with questions, handling family reactions, and staying patient in difficult times are all integral aspects of a believer's journey. By turning to the Quran, the teachings of the Prophet ﷺ, and the insights of Islamic scholars, we can navigate these challenges with wisdom and faith. Each situation is an opportunity to strengthen our relationship with Allah and grow in our understanding of His divine plan.

Chapter 14:

The Power of Du'a (Supplication) and Dhikr (Remembrance of Allah)

1. Du'as Every Muslim Should Know

Du'a, or supplication, is one of the most powerful acts of worship in Islam, as it establishes a direct connection between the believer and Allah. It is a profound expression of faith, humility, and reliance on the Creator. The Prophet Muhammad ﷺ emphasized the importance of du'a, saying,

> **"Du'a is worship." (Sunan Abi Dawud)**

This hadith underscores that du'a is not merely a request but an act of devotion that demonstrates a believer's acknowledgment of Allah's power and mercy. Every Muslim should memorize and recite key du'as from the Quran and Sunnah, as they encompass all aspects of life, from seeking guidance to asking for forgiveness and protection.

One of the most comprehensive du'as is:

> **"Our Lord, give us in this world [that which is] good and in the Hereafter [that which is] good and protect us from the punishment of the Fire." (Quran 2:201)**

This du'a, taught in the Quran, is a beautiful example of how believers should seek both worldly and spiritual blessings. Another essential du'a is for seeking forgiveness:

> **"Our Lord, we have wronged ourselves, and if You do not forgive us and have mercy upon us, we will surely be among the losers."** **(Quran 7:23)**

This verse reflects the humility and self-awareness required in du'a, as it acknowledges human fallibility and the need for divine mercy.

Scholars like Ibn Taymiyyah explain that du'a is a manifestation of a servant's humility and dependence on Allah. It is a means of drawing closer to Him and seeking His assistance in all matters. The Prophet ﷺ also taught specific du'as for various situations, such as the du'a for entering and leaving the home, eating, traveling, and even during times of distress. For instance, the du'a for anxiety is:

> **"O Allah, I seek refuge in You from grief and sadness, from weakness and laziness, from miserliness and cowardice, and from being overwhelmed by debt and the oppression of men."** **(Sahih al-Bukhari)**

By incorporating these du'as into daily life, Muslims can ensure they are constantly connected to Allah and seeking His guidance and protection.

2. The Benefits of Remembering Allah Daily

Remembering Allah (dhikr) is a profound act of worship that brings immense spiritual, emotional, and psychological benefits. It is a means of purifying the heart, strengthening faith, and maintaining a constant awareness of Allah's presence. Allah says in the Quran:

> **"Verily, in the remembrance of Allah do hearts find rest."** **(Quran**

13:28)

This verse highlights the tranquility and peace that come from engaging in dhikr, as it reminds believers of Allah's greatness and their reliance on Him.

The Prophet Muhammad ﷺ emphasized the importance of dhikr in numerous hadiths. He said:

> **"The example of the one who remembers Allah and the one who does not is like the example of the living and the dead."** (Sahih al-Bukhari)

This analogy illustrates the transformative power of dhikr, as it brings spiritual life to the heart and soul. Daily dhikr, such as reciting *SubhanAllah* (Glory be to Allah), *Alhamdulillah* (All praise is due to Allah), and *Allahu Akbar* (Allah is the Greatest), serves as a constant reminder of Allah's attributes and blessings.

Scholars like Imam al-Ghazali have written extensively about the benefits of dhikr. They explain that consistent remembrance of Allah purifies the heart, removes distractions, and strengthens one's connection to the Creator. Dhikr also serves as a shield against sin, as it keeps the believer mindful of Allah's presence and His commandments. The Prophet ﷺ said:

> **"Shall I not inform you of the best of your deeds, the purest in the sight of your Lord, and the highest in rank—better than giving gold and silver, and better than meeting your enemies in battle where you strike their necks and they strike yours? It is the remembrance of Allah."** (Sunan al-Tirmidhi)

This hadith underscores the immense reward and spiritual elevation that come from engaging in dhikr.

Moreover, specific forms of dhikr, such as *La ilaha illallah* (There is no god but Allah) and *Astaghfirullah* (I seek forgiveness from Allah), have unique virtues. The Prophet ﷺ said:

"The best dhikr is La ilaha illallah, and the best supplication is Alhamdulillah." (Sunan Ibn Majah)

By incorporating dhikr into daily routines, Muslims can experience the profound benefits of inner peace, increased faith, and a stronger connection to Allah.

3. How to Make Du'a Effectively

Making du'a effectively requires sincerity, humility, and adherence to the etiquette taught in the Quran and Sunnah. It is not merely a ritual but a heartfelt conversation with Allah. Allah says:

"Call upon Me; I will respond to you." (Quran 40:60)

This verse is a powerful reminder of Allah's promise to answer the supplications of His servants. However, for du'a to be effective, it must be made with the proper etiquette and conditions.

The Prophet Muhammad ﷺ taught specific etiquettes for du'a, such as beginning with praising Allah and sending blessings upon the Prophet ﷺ. He said:

"When any one of you makes du'a, let him start by praising Allah and then send blessings upon the Prophet ﷺ, then let him ask for whatever he wants." (Sunan al-Tirmidhi)

This approach ensures that the du'a begins with humility and gratitude, acknowledging Allah's greatness and the Prophet's role as a guide.

Another key aspect of effective du'a is to ask with conviction and certainty. The Prophet ﷺ said:

"Call upon Allah while being certain of being answered, and know that Allah does not respond to a du'a from a distracted heart."

(Sunan al-Tirmidhi)

This hadith emphasizes the importance of focus and sincerity in du'a. A distracted or half-hearted du'a is less likely to be answered, as it lacks the necessary devotion and trust in Allah's power.

Scholars like Ibn al-Qayyim have elaborated on the conditions for effective du'a. They highlight the importance of persistence, as delays in response may be a test or a means of increasing the believer's reward. The Prophet ﷺ said:

> **"The du'a of any one of you will be answered so long as he is not impatient and says, 'I made du'a but it was not answered.'" (Sahih al-Bukhari)**

This teaches believers to remain patient and steadfast, trusting in Allah's wisdom and timing.

Additionally, du'a should be made at times when it is more likely to be accepted, such as during the last third of the night, while prostrating in prayer, or between the adhan and iqamah. The Prophet ﷺ said:

> **"The closest a servant is to his Lord is when he is in prostration, so increase your du'a in it." (Sahih Muslim)**

By observing these etiquettes and conditions, Muslims can ensure their du'as are more impactful and aligned with the teachings of Islam.

In conclusion, du'a and dhikr are essential acts of worship that strengthen a believer's relationship with Allah. By learning key du'as, engaging in daily dhikr, and making du'a effectively, Muslims can experience the profound spiritual benefits of these practices and draw closer to their Creator.

Chapter 15:

Finding a Muslim Community

1. Why Muslim Brotherhood/Sisterhood is Important

The concept of Muslim brotherhood and sisterhood is a cornerstone of Islamic teachings, emphasizing unity, compassion, and mutual support among believers. Allah (SWT) says in the Quran:

> "The believers are but brothers, so make settlement between your brothers. And fear Allah that you may receive mercy." (Quran 49:10)

This verse highlights the spiritual bond that ties Muslims together, transcending race, nationality, and social status. It establishes that the relationship between Muslims is not merely social or cultural but rooted in faith and shared devotion to Allah. The Prophet Muhammad ﷺ further reinforced this idea in a hadith:

> "The believers, in their mutual kindness, compassion, and sympathy, are like one body. If one part of the body feels pain, the whole body responds to it with wakefulness and fever." (Sahih Bukhari and Muslim)

This analogy illustrates the profound interconnectedness of the Muslim community. When one member suffers, the entire ummah is called to respond with empathy and action. Scholars like Imam Ibn Taymiyyah have explained that this brotherhood is not merely a social construct but a divine obligation rooted in faith. It fosters a sense of belonging, strengthens communal ties, and ensures that Muslims support one another in times of need.

The Prophet ﷺ also said:

> **"None of you truly believes until he loves for his brother what he loves for himself." (Sahih Bukhari and Muslim)**

This hadith underscores the selflessness and empathy that should define Muslim relationships. Scholars such as Imam Al-Ghazali have elaborated on this principle, stating that true brotherhood in Islam requires sincerity, sacrifice, and a commitment to the well-being of others. By upholding this principle, Muslims fulfill a key aspect of their faith and contribute to a harmonious society. The brotherhood/sisterhood in Islam is not limited to personal relationships but extends to the global Muslim community, reminding believers of their shared responsibility to uphold justice, support the oppressed, and spread goodness.

2.How to Find a Masjid or Islamic Center

Finding a masjid or Islamic center is essential for Muslims to connect with their community, perform congregational prayers, and seek knowledge. Allah (SWT) encourages gathering in His remembrance:

> **"In houses which Allah has ordered to be raised and in which His name is remembered, there exalt Him therein, in the mornings and the evenings, men whom neither commerce nor sale distracts from the remembrance of Allah." (Quran 24:36-37)**

This verse highlights the sanctity of masjids as places where believers come together to worship and strengthen their connection with Allah. The Prophet Muhammad ﷺ also emphasized the importance of attending the masjid:

"Whoever goes to the mosque in the morning or evening, Allah prepares for him a place in Paradise every time he goes or comes." (Sahih Bukhari and Muslim)

This hadith demonstrates the immense spiritual rewards associated with visiting the masjid. To locate a masjid, one can use online resources such as Islamic directories, apps like "Muslim Pro" or "Salatuk," or local Muslim networks. Social media platforms and community boards often provide information about nearby Islamic centers. Additionally, reaching out to local Muslim organizations or asking fellow Muslims for recommendations can be helpful.

Scholars like Imam Al-Ghazali have stressed the significance of the masjid as a place of spiritual growth and community bonding. In his works, he describes the masjid as a sanctuary where believers can escape the distractions of the world and focus on their relationship with Allah. Visiting a masjid not only fulfills religious duties but also helps Muslims build relationships, gain a deeper understanding of their faith, and participate in communal activities such as Quran classes, lectures, and charitable initiatives.

The Prophet ﷺ also said:

"When three people are in a village or desert and they do not establish prayer together, then Satan has overcome them. So, observe prayer in congregation, for the wolf eats only the stray sheep." (Sunan Abu Dawood)

This hadith emphasizes the importance of congregational prayer and the dangers of isolating oneself from the Muslim community. By finding and attending a masjid, Muslims can strengthen their faith, foster unity, and fulfill the Sunnah of the Prophet ﷺ.

3. Building Friendships with Fellow Muslims

Building friendships with fellow Muslims is a vital aspect of Islamic life, as it strengthens faith and fosters a sense of unity. The Quran reminds us:

> **"And hold firmly to the rope of Allah all together and do not become divided." (Quran 3:103)**

This verse calls Muslims to unite and avoid division, highlighting the importance of strong, faith-based relationships. The Prophet Muhammad ﷺ also highlighted the importance of good companionship:

> **"A person is upon the religion of their close friend, so let one of you look at whom they befriend." (Sunan Abu Dawood)**

This hadith serves as a reminder that the company we keep has a profound impact on our faith and character. Scholars like Imam Nawawi have explained that righteous friendships encourage good deeds, provide emotional support, and help Muslims stay steadfast in their faith. In his famous work *Riyad al-Salihin*, Imam Nawawi dedicates an entire chapter to the virtues of good companionship, emphasizing its role in spiritual growth.

To build such friendships, one should actively participate in community events, engage in acts of kindness, and seek out individuals who embody Islamic values. The Prophet ﷺ said:

> **"The example of a good companion and a bad companion is like that of a seller of musk and a blacksmith. The seller of musk will either give you some perfume, or you will buy some from him, or you will notice a pleasant smell from him. As for the blacksmith, he will either burn your clothes, or you will notice a bad smell from him." (Sahih Bukhari and Muslim)**

This analogy illustrates the influence of friends on one's character and faith.

A righteous friend inspires goodness, while a negative companion can lead one astray. Scholars like Ibn Qayyim al-Jawziyya have also emphasized the importance of choosing friends who remind us of Allah and encourage us to strive for excellence in both worldly and spiritual matters.

In addition to choosing good friends, Muslims should strive to be good friends themselves. The Prophet ﷺ said:

"The most beloved of people to Allah are those who are most beneficial to people." (Al-Mu'jam al-Awsat)

By being kind, supportive, and sincere, Muslims can build lasting friendships that strengthen the ummah and bring them closer to Allah. These relationships are not only a source of joy in this life but also a means of attaining Allah's pleasure and reward in the hereafter.

Part 4:
Family, Society, and Challenges

Chapter 16:

Islam and Family Life

1. The Importance of Family in Islam

The family is the cornerstone of Islamic society, serving as the foundation for moral, spiritual, and social development. Islam places immense emphasis on the sanctity of family ties, as they are integral to maintaining a balanced and harmonious community. The Quran and Sunnah provide clear guidance on the importance of family, emphasizing love, mercy, and mutual respect among its members. Allah says in the Quran:

> **"And it is He who has created man from water and has made for him relationships by blood and marriage, for your Lord is ever Powerful." (Quran 25:54)**

This verse highlights the divine wisdom behind the creation of familial bonds. The Prophet Muhammad ﷺ further emphasized the significance of maintaining family ties, stating:

> **"Whoever believes in Allah and the Last Day, let him maintain the bonds of kinship." (Sahih Bukhari)**

 The Power of Du'a (Supplication) and Dhikr (Remembrance of Allah)⊠
Scholars like Ibn Kathir explain that maintaining family ties is not only a means of earning Allah's pleasure but also a way to ensure societal stability. The family unit is where individuals learn values such as compassion, respon-

sibility, and faith, which are essential for a thriving Muslim community.

2. Rights and Responsibilities of Parents and Children

In Islam, the relationship between parents and children is governed by a set of rights and responsibilities that ensure mutual respect and care. Parents are entrusted with the upbringing of their children in accordance with Islamic principles, while children are obligated to honor and obey their parents. Allah commands in the Quran:

> **"And your Lord has decreed that you worship none but Him, and that you be kind to parents. Whether one or both of them reach old age in your life, say not to them a word of disrespect, nor shout at them, but address them in terms of honor."**
> **(Quran 17:23)**

This verse underscores the importance of treating parents with kindness and respect, even in challenging circumstances. The Prophet Muhammad ﷺ also highlighted the significance of fulfilling parental rights, stating:

> **"Paradise lies at the feet of your mother."** **(Sunan An-Nasa'i)**

Scholars such as Imam Al-Ghazali explain that the rights of parents include providing for their children's physical, emotional, and spiritual needs, while children must reciprocate with gratitude and care, especially as their parents age. This reciprocal relationship fosters a sense of duty and love within the family.

3. Building a Strong Muslim Household

A strong Muslim household is built on the principles of faith, mutual respect, and adherence to Islamic teachings. The Quran and Sunnah provide a comprehensive framework for creating a home that is a sanctuary of peace and spirituality. Allah says in the Quran:

> **"And Allah has made for you from your homes a place of rest."**
> **(Quran 16:80)**

This verse highlights the importance of the home as a place of comfort and tranquility. The Prophet Muhammad ﷺ emphasized the role of both spouses in maintaining a harmonious household, stating:

> **"The best of you is the one who is best to his family, and I am the**
> **best of you to my family." (Sunan At-Tirmidhi)**

Scholars like Ibn Al-Qayyim have elaborated on the importance of fostering an environment of love, patience, and understanding within the family. This includes regular acts of worship, such as praying together, reading the Quran, and engaging in dhikr, as well as resolving conflicts with wisdom and compassion. A strong Muslim household is one where Islamic values are lived and practiced daily, creating a nurturing environment for all members.

By adhering to these principles, Muslim families can fulfill their roles as the building blocks of a righteous society, earning the pleasure of Allah and contributing to the well-being of the Ummah.

Chapter 17:

Marriage in Islam

1. Finding a Spouse the Islamic Way

In Islam, finding a spouse is a sacred process guided by divine principles. The Quran emphasizes the importance of choosing a righteous partner, stating:

> **"And marry the unmarried among you and the righteous among your male slaves and female slaves. If they should be poor, Allah will enrich them from His bounty, and Allah is all-Encompassing and Knowing." (Quran 24:32)**

The Prophet Muhammad ﷺ also highlighted the significance of choosing a spouse based on piety and character. He said:

> **"A woman is married for four things: her wealth, her lineage, her beauty, and her religion. So, marry the one who is religious, may your hands be rubbed with dust (i.e., may you prosper)." (Sahih al-Bukhari)**

Scholars like Ibn Kathir explain that this hadith underscores the importance of prioritizing faith over worldly attributes. The process of finding a spouse should involve sincere prayer (Istikhara), consultation with family, and adherence to Islamic guidelines to ensure compatibility and shared values.

2. The Role of Husband and Wife

Islam defines clear and complementary roles for husbands and wives, fostering harmony and mutual respect in marriage. The Quran describes the relationship between spouses as one of mercy and tranquility:

> **"And of His signs is that He created for you from yourselves mates that you may find tranquility in them; and He placed between you affection and mercy. Indeed, in that are signs for a people who give thought." (Quran 30:21)**

The husband is designated as the protector and maintainer of the family, as stated in the Quran:

> **"Men are in charge of women by [right of] what Allah has given one over the other and what they spend [for maintenance] from their wealth." (Quran 4:34)**

However, this leadership is not authoritarian but rooted in kindness and consultation. The Prophet Muhammad ﷺ said:

> **"The best of you are those who are best to their wives, and I am the best of you to my wives." (Sunan Ibn Majah)**

Wives, on the other hand, are encouraged to be supportive and nurturing. Scholars like Imam Al-Ghazali emphasize that a wife's role is to create a peaceful home environment, while both partners are expected to cooperate and fulfill each other's rights with love and respect.

3. How to Maintain a Happy Islamic Marriage

Maintaining a happy Islamic marriage requires continuous effort, patience, and adherence to Islamic teachings. The Quran advises spouses to treat each other with kindness and fairness:

> **"And live with them in kindness. For if you dislike them – perhaps you dislike a thing and Allah makes therein much good." (Quran 4:19)**

The Prophet Muhammad ﷺ emphasized the importance of good character and communication in marriage. He said:

> **"The most perfect believer in faith is the one who is best in character, and the best of you are those who are best to their wives." (Sunan al-Tirmidhi)**

Scholars like Ibn Qayyim Al-Jawziyya highlight that maintaining a happy marriage involves fulfilling each other's emotional, physical, and spiritual needs. Regular acts of kindness, expressing gratitude, and resolving conflicts through mutual consultation are essential. Additionally, the Prophet ﷺ encouraged playful interactions with one's spouse, saying:

> **"Everything in which there is no remembrance of Allah is idle play except four things: a man playing with his wife..." (Sunan al-Nasa'i)**

By following these guidelines, couples can build a strong, loving, and lasting relationship that pleases Allah and serves as a foundation for a righteous family.

Chapter 18:

Living as a Muslim in a Non-Muslim Society

1. Practicing Islam in a Non-Muslim Environment

Practicing Islam in a non–Muslim environment can be challenging, but it is also an opportunity to demonstrate the beauty and resilience of faith. The Quran reminds Muslims to remain steadfast in their beliefs while maintaining good conduct:

> **"So remain on a right course as you have been commanded, [you] and those who have turned back with you [to Allah], and do not transgress. Indeed, He is Seeing of what you do." (Quran 11:112)**

This verse emphasizes the importance of staying consistent in worship and moral conduct, even when surrounded by differing beliefs. The Prophet Muhammad ﷺ also provided guidance for such situations. In a hadith, he said:

> **"Whoever among you sees an evil, let him change it with his hand; if he cannot, then with his tongue; if he cannot, then with his heart—and that is the weakest of faith." (Sahih Muslim)**

This teaches Muslims to uphold their values while respecting the environment they are in.   Scholars like Ibn Taymiyyah have explained that Muslims should strive to balance their religious obligations with the realities of their surroundings, ensuring that their actions reflect the mercy and wisdom of Islam. For example, finding quiet spaces for prayer, adhering to halal dietary restrictions, and dressing modestly are ways to practice Islam without causing unnecessary conflict.

2. How to Deal with Workplace Challenges

Navigating workplace challenges as a Muslim requires patience, integrity, and a strong sense of ethics. The Quran encourages believers to act justly and with excellence in all aspects of life:

> **"Indeed, Allah commands you to uphold justice and to do good and to give to relatives. And He forbids immorality and bad conduct and oppression. He admonishes you that perhaps you will be reminded." (Quran 16:90)**

This verse highlights the importance of fairness and kindness, even in difficult situations. The Prophet Muhammad ﷺ also emphasized the value of honesty and hard work. He said:

> **"The truthful and trustworthy merchant will be with the prophets, the truthful, and the martyrs." (Sunan al-Tirmidhi)**

This hadith underscores the significance of integrity in professional life. Scholars like Imam Al-Ghazali have elaborated on the concept of *ikhlas* (sincerity), advising Muslims to perform their duties with the intention of pleasing Allah, regardless of the challenges they face. For instance, dealing with workplace discrimination or balancing religious obligations like prayer times can be managed through open communication and time management, ensuring that one's faith and professional responsibilities are both upheld.

3. Respecting Others While Maintaining Your Faith

Respecting others while maintaining your faith is a cornerstone of Islamic teachings. The Quran emphasizes the importance of kindness and respect for all people, regardless of their beliefs:

> **"Allah does not forbid you from those who do not fight you because of religion and do not expel you from your homes—from being righteous toward them and acting justly toward them. Indeed, Allah loves those who act justly." (Quran 60:8)**

This verse encourages Muslims to treat others with fairness and compassion, even when their beliefs differ. The Prophet Muhammad ﷺ exemplified this principle in his interactions with non-Muslims. He said:

> **"Whoever harms a non-Muslim under Muslim protection, I will be his adversary on the Day of Judgment." (Sunan al-Kubra)**

This hadith highlights the importance of honoring agreements and treating others with dignity. Scholars like Yusuf al-Qaradawi have explained that respecting others does not mean compromising one's faith; rather, it means engaging in dialogue and coexistence with wisdom and kindness. For example, explaining Islamic practices to colleagues or neighbors in a respectful manner can foster mutual understanding while maintaining religious integrity.

By adhering to these principles, Muslims can navigate non-Muslim environments, workplace challenges, and interactions with others in a way that upholds their faith while promoting harmony and respect. The Quran, hadith, and scholarly explanations provide a comprehensive framework for balancing religious obligations with the demands of daily life.

Chapter 19:

Common Misconceptions About Islam

1. Islam and Women's Rights

Islam has long been a subject of debate regarding its stance on women's rights. Contrary to popular misconceptions, Islam grants women significant rights and dignity. The Quran explicitly states the equality of men and women in spiritual and moral responsibilities:

> **"Indeed, the Muslim men and Muslim women, the believing men and believing women, the obedient men and obedient women, the truthful men and truthful women, the patient men and patient women, the humble men and humble women, the charitable men and charitable women, the fasting men and fasting women, the men who guard their private parts and the women who do so, and the men who remember Allah often and the women who do so – for them Allah has prepared forgiveness and a great reward."**
> **(Quran 33:35)**

This verse underscores that both genders are equally valued in the eyes of Allah. Additionally, Islam granted women the right to inherit, own property, and seek education centuries before many other societies. The Prophet Muhammad ﷺ emphasized the importance of treating women with kindness and respect, stating:

> "The best among you are those who are best to their wives."
> (Sunan Ibn Majah)

Scholars like Ibn Kathir and contemporary thinkers such as Dr. Ingrid Mattson have highlighted how Islamic teachings elevated women's status in a patriarchal society, ensuring their rights in marriage, divorce, and financial independence.

2. Does Islam Promote Violence?

The question of whether Islam promotes violence is often rooted in misunderstandings and misrepresentations of its teachings. The Quran explicitly condemns unjust aggression and emphasizes peace:

> "And do not kill the soul which Allah has forbidden, except by right. And whoever is killed unjustly, we have given his heir authority, but let him not exceed limits in taking life. Indeed, he will be supported." (Quran 17:33)

Furthermore, the Prophet Muhammad ﷺ taught that harming innocent people is a grave sin:

> "Whoever kills a person [unjustly]... it is as if he had killed all mankind." (Quran 5:32)

Scholars like Imam Al-Ghazali and contemporary figures such as Sheikh Hamza Yusuf have clarified that Islam permits self-defense and just war only under strict conditions, such as protecting the oppressed or defending against aggression. The concept of *qital* (fighting) in Islam is heavily regulated and not synonymous with violence. The Prophet Muhammad ﷺ also said:

"Do not wish to meet the enemy, but if you encounter them, be steadfast." (Sahih Bukhari)

This indicates that violence is not encouraged but is a last resort in specific circumstances.

3. Clearing Up Misunderstandings About Jihad

The term *jihad* is often misrepresented as synonymous with holy war or violence. In reality, jihad encompasses a broader spiritual and moral struggle. The Quran describes the greater jihad (*jihad al-akbar*) as the struggle against one's own desires and shortcomings:

"And strive for Allah with the striving due to Him." (Quran 22:78)

The lesser jihad (*jihad al-asghar*) refers to physical struggle, which is strictly regulated and only permissible in self-defense or to protect the oppressed. The Prophet Muhammad ﷺ said:

"The best jihad is a word of truth spoken before a tyrannical ruler." (Sunan Ibn Majah)

This highlights that speaking truth to power is a form of jihad. Scholars like Ibn Taymiyyah and modern interpreters such as Dr. Tariq Ramadan have emphasized that jihad is not a call to violence but a call to uphold justice and righteousness. The Quran also states:

"And if they incline to peace, then incline to it and rely upon Allah." (Quran 8:61)

This verse underscores that peace is always the preferred outcome, and violence is only a last resort.

By examining these teachings, it becomes clear that Islam advocates for women's rights, condemns unjust violence, and defines jihad as a multifaceted struggle for justice and self-improvement. Misunderstandings often arise from taking verses or hadith out of context, but a holistic understanding reveals Islam's emphasis on peace, justice, and equality.

Chapter 20:

Facing Islamophobia and Staying Strong

1. Dealing with Discrimination

Discrimination is a painful reality that many face, but Islam provides profound guidance on how to navigate such challenges with patience, dignity, and faith. The Quran reminds us that trials are a part of life, and how we respond to them defines our character. Allah says,

> "And We will surely test you with something of fear and hunger and a loss of wealth and lives and fruits, but give good tidings to the patient." (Quran 2:155)

This verse emphasizes that hardships, including discrimination, are tests from Allah, and patience is key to overcoming them. The Prophet Muhammad ﷺ also faced immense discrimination and persecution in Mecca, yet he responded with compassion and resilience. A hadith narrated by Muslim states,

> "The believer who mixes with people and endures their harm is better than the one who does not mix with them nor endure their harm."

This teaches us that enduring hardship while maintaining good character is a sign of strong faith. Scholars like Ibn Taymiyyah explain that facing discrimination with patience and trust in Allah's plan elevates a believer's status and purifies their soul. By turning to Allah in prayer and seeking strength through faith, Muslims can rise above discrimination and remain steadfast in their principles.

2. How to Respond to Hate and Criticism

In a world where hate and criticism are prevalent, Islam teaches Muslims to respond with wisdom, kindness, and integrity. The Quran advises,

> **"Repel evil with that which is better, and then the one who is hostile to you will become as a devoted friend." (Quran 41:34)**

This verse encourages responding to negativity with positivity, as it has the power to transform animosity into harmony. The Prophet Muhammad ﷺ exemplified this principle when he was ridiculed and insulted by the people of Ta'if. Instead of retaliating, he prayed for their guidance, saying,

> **"O Allah, guide my people, for they do not know."**

This demonstrates the importance of responding to hate with compassion and a desire for the betterment of others. Scholars like Imam Al-Ghazali emphasize that reacting to criticism with anger only fuels conflict, while responding with patience and wisdom reflects true Islamic character. By focusing on self-improvement and seeking Allah's pleasure, Muslims can rise above hate and criticism, turning challenges into opportunities for spiritual growth.

3. Being a Proud Muslim in Today's World

Being a proud Muslim in today's world means embracing one's identity with confidence, while adhering to the teachings of Islam and contributing positively to society. The Quran affirms,

> **"This day I have perfected for you your religion and completed My favor upon you and have approved for you Islam as religion."**
> **(Quran 5:3)**

This verse reminds Muslims that Islam is a complete and perfect way of life, worthy of pride and dedication. The Prophet Muhammad ﷺ said,

> **"The believer is like a firm mountain; he does not waver."**

This hadith encourages Muslims to stand firm in their faith, even in the face of societal pressures or misconceptions about Islam. Scholars like Yusuf Al-Qaradawi highlight that being a proud Muslim does not mean arrogance, but rather a deep sense of gratitude and responsibility to represent Islam with excellence. By embodying the values of honesty, kindness, and justice, Muslims can showcase the beauty of their faith and inspire others. In a world that often misunderstands Islam, being a proud Muslim means being a beacon of light, guided by the Quran and Sunnah, and striving to make a positive impact on humanity.

Part 5:
Continuing Your Journey

Chapter 21:

Developing a Routine as a New Muslim

1. How to Establish an Islamic Routine

Establishing an Islamic routine involves integrating acts of worship and virtuous deeds into your daily life. This routine should be structured around the five daily prayers, which are the foundation of a Muslim's connection with Allah. The Prophet Muhammad ﷺ emphasized the importance of consistency in worship, as narrated in the hadith:

> "The most beloved deeds to Allah are those that are consistent, even if they are small." (Sahih al-Bukhari and Sahih Muslim)

Begin your day with the remembrance of Allah, as mentioned in the Quran:

> "And remember your Lord within yourself in humility and in fear without being apparent in speech - in the mornings and the evenings. And do not be among the heedless."
> (Quran 7:205)

Scholars like Imam Al-Ghazali have emphasized the significance of a structured routine, suggesting that it helps in maintaining spiritual focus and discipline. Incorporate practices such as reciting the Quran, making dua, and engaging in charitable acts regularly. Set aside specific times for learning and reflecting on Islamic knowledge to deepen your understanding and strengthen your faith.

2. Creating Daily and Weekly Goals

Setting daily and weekly goals is essential for personal growth and spiritual development. These goals should align with Islamic principles and help you become a better Muslim. Start by identifying areas of improvement, such as increasing your knowledge of Islam, enhancing your character, or improving your acts of worship. The Quran encourages believers to strive for excellence:

> **"And say, 'My Lord, increase me in knowledge.'" (Quran 20:114)**

Create a list of achievable goals and break them down into smaller, manageable tasks. For example, aim to memorize a new surah each week or perform voluntary fasts on Mondays and Thursdays, as recommended by the Prophet ﷺ:

> **"Fasting three days of each month is equivalent to fasting the entire year." (Sahih al-Bukhari and Sahih Muslim)**

Scholars advise that setting realistic goals and tracking your progress can motivate you to stay committed. Regularly review and adjust your goals to ensure they remain relevant and challenging.

3. Staying Consistent in Worship

Consistency in worship is key to spiritual growth and maintaining a strong connection with Allah. It requires dedication, discipline, and a sincere intention to please Allah. The Quran highlights the importance of steadfastness:

> **"And worship your Lord until there comes to you the certainty (death)."**

(Quran 15:99)

The Prophet Muhammad ﷺ set an exemplary model of consistency in worship. He would often emphasize the rewards of continuous good deeds, even if they are small. One of the most profound hadiths on this subject is:

"Take up good deeds only as much as you are able, for the best deeds are those done regularly even if they are few." (Sunan Ibn Majah)

Scholars like Ibn Qayyim Al-Jawziyyah have discussed the concept of "Muraqaba," or mindfulness in worship, which helps in maintaining consistency. They advise focusing on the quality of your worship rather than the quantity. Engage in acts of worship with full concentration and sincerity, and seek Allah's help in staying consistent. Remember that Allah is always watching and is pleased with those who strive to worship Him consistently.

In conclusion, establishing an Islamic routine, setting achievable goals, and maintaining consistency in worship are essential for spiritual growth. By following the guidance of the Quran, the Sunnah of the Prophet ﷺ, and the insights of Islamic scholars, you can cultivate a life that is pleasing to Allah and beneficial for your personal development.

Chapter 22:

Recommended Books and Resources

1. Essential Books for New Muslims

For new Muslims, building a strong foundation in Islamic knowledge is crucial, and certain books serve as essential guides. "The Quran: A Translation" by Abdullah Yusuf Ali or Saheeh International is indispensable, as the Quran is the primary source of Islamic teachings. Allah says in the Quran:

> **"This is the Book about which there is no doubt, a guidance for those conscious of Allah."** **(Quran 2:2)**

Another vital resource is *"Riyad as-Salihin"* by Imam Nawawi, a compilation of hadiths that cover various aspects of life, from worship to character. The Prophet Muhammad ﷺ said:

> **"I have left among you two things; you will never go astray as long as you hold fast to them: the Book of Allah and my Sunnah."** **(Hadith, Al-Muwatta)**

For understanding the basics of faith, *"The Fundamentals of Tawheed"* by Dr. Abu Ameenah Bilal Philips is highly recommended. Scholars like Ibn Taymiyyah emphasize the importance of Tawheed, stating that it is the essence of Islam. Additionally, *"The Sealed Nectar"* by Safiur Rahman Mubarakpuri provides an in-depth biography of the Prophet Muhammad ﷺ, offering insights into his life and teachings. These books, combined with consistent study and reflection, help new Muslims strengthen their faith and understanding of Islam.

2. Useful Websites and Apps

In the digital age, numerous websites and apps provide reliable Islamic knowledge for new Muslims. Websites like **IslamQA.info**, supervised by Sheikh Muhammad Saalih al-Munajjid, offer detailed answers to Islamic questions based on the Quran and Sunnah. Another trusted platform is **Bayyinah.tv**, founded by Nouman Ali Khan, which provides Quranic Arabic courses and tafsir (exegesis) lessons. For hadith studies, **Sunnah.com** is an excellent resource, offering access to authentic hadith collections like Sahih al-Bukhari and Sahih Muslim.

Apps such as **Muslim Pro** assist with daily prayers, Quran recitation, and Islamic reminders. The Quran app by **quran.com** is user-friendly and provides translations in multiple languages. The Prophet Muhammad ﷺ encouraged seeking knowledge:

> **"Whoever treads a path in search of knowledge, Allah will make easy for him the path to Paradise."** (Hadith, Sahih Muslim)

These digital tools, when used responsibly, can greatly enhance a new Muslim's journey of learning and practicing Islam.

3. Trusted Islamic Scholars and Speakers

Learning from trusted Islamic scholars ensures that new Muslims receive accurate and authentic knowledge. Scholars like **Sheikh Ibn Uthaymeen**, known for his extensive works on Tawheed and Fiqh, provide clear explanations of Islamic principles. His commentary on *"The Three Fundamental Principles"* is highly recommended for beginners. Another renowned scholar, **Sheikh Yusuf Al-Qaradawi**, has written extensively on contemporary issues, helping Muslims navigate modern challenges while staying true to Islamic teachings.

In the English-speaking world, **Nouman Ali Khan** is widely respected for his Quranic tafsir and engaging lectures. Similarly, **Dr. Zakir Naik** is known for his comparative religion talks, which help new Muslims understand Islam in the context of other faiths. The Prophet Muhammad ﷺ said:

> **"The scholars are the inheritors of the Prophets."** (Hadith, Sunan Abi Dawud)

This highlights the importance of seeking knowledge from qualified scholars. By following the teachings of these trusted figures, new Muslims can gain a deeper understanding of Islam and avoid misconceptions.

Chapter 23:

Learning Arabic for Worship

1. Why Learning Arabic is Important

Learning Arabic is a profoundly enriching experience that offers numerous benefits, particularly for Muslims. As the language of the Quran, Arabic allows individuals to engage directly with the divine revelations, fostering a deeper understanding and appreciation of Islamic teachings. The Quran, revealed in Arabic, is considered a linguistic miracle, and its eloquence and beauty are best appreciated in the original language.

> **"Indeed, We have sent it down as an Arabic Qur'an that you might understand."**
> **(Quran 12:2)**

For Muslims, understanding Arabic is not just about comprehending the literal meanings of the Quranic verses but also about grasping the subtle nuances and the rich tapestry of meanings woven into the text. This understanding is crucial for spiritual growth and for fulfilling religious obligations accurately.

Moreover, Arabic is the language of Hadith, the sayings and actions of the Prophet Muhammad (PBUH), which provide guidance on various aspects of life. Hadith literature is vast and covers topics ranging from worship and ethics to social interactions and legal matters. Scholars have emphasized the importance of learning Arabic to accurately interpret these texts and avoid misinterpretations that can arise from translations. Imam Al-Shafi'i, a renowned Islamic scholar, stated, "Knowledge of Arabic is half of knowledge," underscoring the significance of the language in Islamic scholarship.

Learning Arabic also opens doors to a rich cultural heritage. Arabic literature, poetry, and philosophy have significantly influenced world culture and thought. Engaging with these works in their original language provides a deeper appreciation of their artistic and intellectual merit. Furthermore, Arabic is one of the most widely spoken languages in the world, with over 400 million speakers. Proficiency in Arabic can enhance communication and cultural exchange, fostering understanding and cooperation among diverse communities.

2. Basic Arabic Phrases Every Muslim Should Know

For Muslims, knowing basic Arabic phrases is essential for performing daily prayers and understanding fundamental Islamic concepts. These phrases are integral to the practice of Islam and help establish a direct connection with Allah. Some essential phrases include:

- **"Allahu Akbar"** – "God is the Greatest," recited during prayers and various occasions to express faith and submission. This phrase is a testament to the belief in the supremacy of Allah and is used to glorify Him.
- **"Alhamdulillah"** – "Praise be to God," used to express gratitude and appreciation for blessings. It acknowledges that all good comes from Allah and encourages a mindset of thankfulness.
- **"Subhan Allah"** – "Glory be to God," recited to praise Allah and acknowledge His greatness. This phrase is often used to express awe and admiration for the wonders of creation.
- **"Astaghfirullah"** – "I seek forgiveness from God," said to repent and seek Allah's forgiveness. It is a reminder of human fallibility and the need for constant self-improvement.
- **"Insha'Allah"** – "If God wills," used to express hope and acknowledgment that all outcomes are subject to Allah's will. It encourages humility and

trust in divine providence.

The Prophet Muhammad (PBUH) emphasized the importance of these phrases in various Hadith. For instance:

"The Prophet (PBUH) said, 'Whoever says, 'Subhan Allah wa bi-hamdihi,' a hundred times a day, will be forgiven all his sins even if they were as much as the foam of the sea.'" (Sahih al-Bukhari)

These phrases are not just words but powerful invocations that carry spiritual significance. They help Muslims stay connected to their faith throughout the day and cultivate a mindset of devotion, gratitude, and humility.

3. How to Start Learning Arabic

Embarking on the journey to learn Arabic can be both rewarding and enlightening. For beginners, starting with the basics, such as learning the Arabic alphabet and pronunciation rules, is crucial. The Arabic script is unique, and mastering it requires practice and patience. Engaging with native speakers, attending language courses, and utilizing online resources can significantly enhance the learning process. Consistency and practice are key; dedicating time each day to study and practice Arabic will yield better results.

Incorporating Arabic into daily routines can also be beneficial. Reading the Quran with translations, listening to Arabic podcasts, and watching Arabic media can help improve language skills. Scholars recommend starting with simple texts and gradually progressing to more complex materials. Imam Al-Ghazali advised, "Seek knowledge from the cradle to the grave," highlighting the importance of continuous learning.

Learning Arabic is not just about acquiring a new language but also about understanding a rich culture and heritage. It opens doors to a deeper appreciation of Islamic literature, poetry, and history. The journey may be challenging, but the rewards are immense, both spiritually and intellectually. As the famous saying goes, "The ink of the scholar is more sacred than the blood of the martyr," emphasizing the significance of knowledge and learning in Islam.

For those serious about learning Arabic, immersing oneself in an Arabic-speaking environment can be highly beneficial. Traveling to Arab countries, participating in language exchange programs, and engaging with Arabic-speaking communities can provide valuable opportunities for practice and cultural immersion. Additionally, utilizing technology, such as language learning apps and online tutoring platforms, can make the learning process more accessible and engaging.

In conclusion, learning Arabic is a journey that offers numerous benefits, from spiritual growth to cultural enrichment. It is a language that connects Muslims to their faith and opens doors to a rich heritage. With dedication and consistent effort, anyone can master Arabic and reap its rewards.

Chapter 24:

Becoming a Role Model for Others

1. Helping Other Reverts on Their Journey

Embracing Islam is a profound and transformative experience, and for many reverts, the journey is filled with both joy and challenges. Helping other reverts navigate their newfound faith is not only a noble act but also a responsibility that can bring immense rewards. The Quran emphasizes the importance of supporting one another in faith:

> "And cooperate in righteousness and piety, but do not cooperate in sin and aggression." (Quran 5:2)

This verse underscores the significance of unity and cooperation among believers, encouraging them to support each other in acts of goodness. Prophet Muhammad ﷺ also highlighted the importance of community and mutual support:

> "The believers in their mutual kindness, compassion, and sympathy *are just like one body. When one of the limbs suffers, the whole body* responds to it with wakefulness and fever." (Hadith, Sahih al-Bukhari and Muslim)

Scholars explain that this hadith emphasizes the interconnectedness of the Muslim community, where the well-being of one affects all. Helping reverts can take many forms, such as providing emotional support, sharing knowledge, and offering practical assistance. By doing so, we not only strengthen their faith but also enrich our own spiritual journey.

One of the most effective ways to help reverts is by sharing personal experiences and insights. Reverts often face unique challenges, such as adjusting to new cultural practices, dealing with family reactions, and overcoming personal doubts. Sharing stories of how one overcame similar obstacles can provide comfort and inspiration. Additionally, connecting reverts with supportive communities, such as local mosques or online forums, can offer them a sense of belonging and access to valuable resources.

Education plays a crucial role in helping reverts understand and practice their new faith. Organizing study circles, workshops, and mentorship programs can provide structured learning opportunities. Topics such as the fundamentals of Islam, Islamic history, and practical aspects of worship can be particularly beneficial. Moreover, providing access to authentic and reliable Islamic literature can help reverts deepen their understanding and avoid misinformation.

Practical support is equally important. This can include assisting with halal food options, helping with Islamic dress codes, and providing guidance on Islamic finance. Offering support during Ramadan, such as inviting reverts for iftar or providing them with resources for fasting, can also strengthen their connection to the community.

Ultimately, helping reverts is a collective responsibility that requires empathy, patience, and a genuine desire to support their spiritual growth. By fostering a supportive and inclusive environment, the Muslim community can help reverts thrive in their newfound faith and contribute positively to the broader community.

2. Being a Good Example of Islam

Being a good example of Islam is crucial in today's world, where misconceptions and stereotypes abound. Living by the principles of Islam and embodying its values can dispel these misconceptions and attract others to the faith. The Quran advises believers to be role models:

> **"You are the best nation produced [as an example] for mankind. You enjoin what is right and forbid what is wrong and believe in Allah." (Quran 3:110)**

This verse highlights the responsibility of Muslims to exemplify righteousness and moral integrity. Prophet Muhammad ﷺ was the epitome of good character and conduct:

> **"Indeed, in the Messenger of Allah, you have a good example to follow for him who hopes in (the Meeting with) Allah and the Last Day and remembers Allah much." (Quran 33:21)**

Scholars interpret this verse as a call to emulate the Prophet's character, which was marked by kindness, patience, and forgiveness. By adhering to these principles, Muslims can inspire others and demonstrate the true essence of Islam.

One of the key aspects of being a good example is maintaining excellent character and conduct. This includes being honest, trustworthy, and compassionate in all interactions. Muslims should strive to be reliable and consistent in their actions, demonstrating integrity in both personal and professional settings. Additionally, showing respect and kindness to all individuals, regardless of their background or beliefs, can foster a positive image of Islam.

Engaging in community service and charitable activities is another way to exemplify Islamic values. Participating in volunteer work, supporting local charities, and contributing to community initiatives can showcase the compassionate and caring nature of Islam. These actions not only benefit the community but also serve as a practical demonstration of Islamic teachings.

Education and knowledge sharing are essential components of being a good example. Muslims should strive to continuously learn and share their knowledge with others. This can involve teaching about Islamic principles, engaging in interfaith dialogues, and promoting understanding and tolerance. By being well-informed and articulate, Muslims can address misconceptions and provide accurate information about Islam.

Maintaining a balanced and moderate lifestyle is also important. Islam encourages moderation in all aspects of life, including diet, social interactions, and personal habits. By avoiding extremes and adhering to a balanced approach, Muslims can demonstrate the practicality and relevance of Islamic teachings in contemporary society.

Moreover, being a good example involves upholding justice and fairness. Muslims should stand up for the rights of others, promote equality, and condemn injustice. This can involve advocating for social causes, supporting human rights, and working towards a more just and equitable society. By embodying these values, Muslims can inspire others to follow the path of righteousness and contribute positively to the world.

3. How to Inspire Others Through Your Actions

Inspiring others through actions is a powerful way to spread the message of Islam. Actions speak louder than words, and when they are aligned with Islamic teachings, they can have a profound impact. The Quran encourages believers to engage in good deeds:

> **"So race to [all that is] good." (Quran 2:148)**

This verse motivates Muslims to strive for excellence in their actions, whether in personal conduct, community service, or professional endeavors. Prophet Muhammad ﷺ emphasized the importance of actions:

"Actions are judged by intentions, and every person will get the reward according to what he has intended." (Hadith, Sahih al-Bukhari and Muslim)

Scholars explain that this hadith underscores the significance of sincere intentions behind actions. When actions are driven by a genuine desire to please Allah and benefit others, they become a source of inspiration. Whether it's through acts of charity, volunteering, or simply being kind and compassionate, Muslims can inspire others to follow the path of righteousness. By embodying the teachings of Islam in their daily lives, they can create a positive ripple effect that touches the hearts and minds of those around them.

One of the most impactful ways to inspire others is through acts of kindness and generosity. Small gestures, such as helping a neighbor, donating to charity, or volunteering time, can make a significant difference. These actions not only benefit the recipients but also demonstrate the compassionate and caring nature of Islam. Moreover, engaging in community service projects, such as cleaning local parks, organizing food drives, or supporting educational initiatives, can inspire others to contribute to their communities.

Leading by example in professional and personal settings is also crucial. Muslims should strive to excel in their fields, whether in academia, business, or other professions. By demonstrating integrity, hard work, and ethical conduct, they can inspire colleagues and peers to follow suit. Additionally, maintaining a positive and respectful demeanor in personal interactions can foster a supportive and harmonious environment.

Sharing knowledge and wisdom is another way to inspire others. Muslims can organize study circles, workshops, and lectures to share Islamic teachings and promote understanding. Engaging in interfaith dialogues and discussions can also help dispel misconceptions and foster mutual respect. By being open to learning and sharing, Muslims can inspire others to seek knowledge and deepen their understanding of the world.

Moreover, practicing forgiveness and patience in the face of adversity can inspire others. Islam emphasizes the importance of forgiveness, compassion, and resilience. By demonstrating these qualities in daily interactions, Muslims can inspire others to adopt a more forgiving and patient approach to life. This can involve forgiving those who have wronged them, showing patience in difficult situations, and maintaining a positive outlook despite challenges.

Ultimately, inspiring others through actions requires a commitment to living by Islamic principles and embodying its values. By consistently demonstrating kindness, generosity, integrity, and compassion, Muslims can inspire others to follow the path of righteousness and contribute positively to society. Through their actions, they can create a ripple effect that spreads goodness and inspires others to embrace the teachings of Islam.

Chapter 25:

Your Next Steps in Islam

1. How to Keep Growing Spiritually

Spiritual growth is a profound and transformative journey that requires continuous effort and self-reflection. In Islam, this journey is guided by the teachings of the Quran and the Sunnah, which provide a comprehensive framework for personal and spiritual development. One of the cornerstones of spiritual growth is the practice of regular prayer, which serves as a direct connection between the believer and Allah. The Quran emphasizes the importance of prayer in numerous verses, highlighting its role in purifying the heart and cultivating mindfulness:

> "Indeed, I am Allah. There is no deity except Me, so worship Me and establish prayer for My remembrance." (Quran 20:14)

Prayer is not merely a ritualistic act but a means of seeking guidance, forgiveness, and spiritual nourishment. It is a time to reflect on one's actions, seek forgiveness for shortcomings, and express gratitude for the blessings bestowed by Allah. The Prophet Muhammad ﷺ emphasized the significance of prayer in cultivating a strong spiritual foundation. He said:

> "The first thing that will be judged among a person's deeds on the Day of Resurrection is the Prayer. If that is in good order, he will succeed and prosper, but if it is defective, he will fail and lose." (Tirmidhi)

In addition to prayer, engaging in acts of charity and kindness is essential for spiritual growth. Charity purifies the soul, fosters empathy, and strengthens the bond between the believer and the community. The Prophet Muhammad ﷺ encouraged acts of charity, emphasizing their role in bringing one closer to Allah. He said:

"Charity does not decrease wealth." (Muslim)

Scholars like Ibn Qayyim Al-Jawziyya have delved deeply into the concept of spiritual growth, emphasizing the importance of purifying the heart and cultivating virtues such as patience, humility, and gratitude. He believed that true spiritual growth comes from aligning one's intentions with the pleasure of Allah and seeking His forgiveness. Ibn Qayyim Al-Jawziyya wrote extensively about the diseases of the heart and their cures, highlighting the importance of self-reflection and introspection in the spiritual journey.

2. Preparing for the Next Stage of Your Journey

As one progresses on the spiritual path, it is crucial to prepare for the next stages of the journey. This preparation involves deepening one's understanding of Islamic teachings and applying them in daily life. The Quran encourages believers to seek knowledge and reflect on the signs of Allah in the universe, as knowledge is a means of drawing closer to Him:

"And He has subjected to you whatever is in the heavens and whatever is on the earth - all from Him. Indeed, in that are signs for a people who give thought." (Quran 45:13)

Seeking knowledge is not limited to religious texts but encompasses all forms of beneficial knowledge that contribute to personal growth and the betterment of society. The Prophet Muhammad ﷺ emphasized the importance of seeking knowledge, stating:

"Seeking knowledge is an obligation upon every Muslim." (Ibn Majah)

Preparing for the next stage of the spiritual journey also involves cultivating a strong sense of community and supporting fellow believers. The Prophet Muhammad ﷺ emphasized the importance of unity and mutual support within the Muslim community. He said:

> **"The believers in their mutual kindness, compassion, and sympathy** *are just like one body. When one of the limbs suffers, the whole body* **responds to it with wakefulness and fever." (Bukhari and Muslim)**

Scholars like Imam Al-Ghazali have emphasized the importance of purifying the heart and cultivating good character as essential steps in preparing for the next stage of one's spiritual journey. He believed that true spiritual growth comes from aligning one's actions with the teachings of the Quran and the Sunnah. Imam Al-Ghazali's works, such as "Ihya' Ulum al-Din" (The Revival of the Religious Sciences), provide a comprehensive guide to spiritual purification and personal development.

3. Final Words of Encouragement

The journey of spiritual growth is a continuous process that requires perseverance, dedication, and a deep commitment to Islamic teachings. It is essential to remember that Allah is always merciful and forgiving, and He rewards those who strive to improve themselves. The Quran offers words of encouragement to those who seek spiritual growth, reminding them of Allah's infinite mercy and support:

> *"And whoever relies upon Allah - then He is sufficient for him. Indeed,* **Allah will accomplish His purpose. Allah has already set for everything a [decreed] extent." (Quran 65:3)**

The Prophet Muhammad ﷺ also offered words of encouragement to his followers, reminding them of the rewards that await those who persevere in their spiritual journey. He said:

> **"The most beloved of actions to Allah are those that are done consistently, even if they are small." (Bukhari and Muslim)**

Scholars like Ibn Taymiyyah have emphasized the importance of remaining steadfast in one's spiritual journey, even in the face of challenges and difficulties. He believed that true spiritual growth comes from trusting in Allah and seeking His guidance in all matters. Ibn Taymiyyah's teachings highlight the importance of patience, perseverance, and unwavering faith in the face of adversity.

In conclusion, the path to spiritual growth is a lifelong journey that requires continuous effort, self-reflection, and a deep commitment to Islamic teachings. By following the guidance of the Quran and the Sunnah, and by cultivating virtues such as patience, humility, and gratitude, one can continue to grow spiritually and draw closer to Allah. The journey may be challenging, but with perseverance and faith, one can overcome obstacles and achieve spiritual fulfillment.

Conclusion

As you reflect on your journey to Islam, take a moment to appreciate the tremendous transformation you have undergone. Embracing Islam is not merely a change in belief; it is the start of a lifelong journey toward self-discovery, spiritual growth, and a closer relationship with Allah. You have made the courageous decision to seek the truth, and with each step forward, you continue to strengthen your connection with the Creator.

Reflecting on Your Journey to Islam

Reflecting on your journey to Islam is a deeply transformative experience, one that helps you appreciate the monumental changes that have taken place within you since you embraced the faith. Every step you have taken since that pivotal moment is a step toward spiritual growth, understanding, and closeness to Allah. Embracing Islam was not just a decision of the heart, but a conscious commitment to a new way of life—one rooted in faith, devotion, and submission to the will of Allah. For many, this journey begins with curiosity, questions, and an internal search for meaning, and it culminates in the realization that Islam provides answers that bring peace and purpose. As you reflect on this journey, you may recognize the challenges you faced— whether they were external struggles or internal doubts—but remember, these obstacles were part of your test, and overcoming them has made you stronger in your faith. Every prayer, every act of charity, every moment of reflection has contributed to shaping your understanding of Islam. This reflection can help you reaffirm your commitment to the path and remember that it is a lifelong journey. In moments of doubt or hardship, look back on how far you've come. Allah has guided you this far, and He will continue to provide His support, mercy, and guidance throughout your entire life. Reflect on His countless blessings and remember that each step forward, no matter how small, is a step closer to the ultimate goal—earning the pleasure of Allah and eternal success in the Hereafter.

The Continuous Path of Learning

One of the most beautiful aspects of Islam is that it is a continuous path of learning and self-improvement. The Quran, with its timeless wisdom, and the teachings of the Prophet ﷺ, offer endless opportunities to gain knowledge, both spiritual and practical. The moment you accepted Islam, you began a lifelong journey of discovery that extends far beyond just learning how to pray or understanding the core beliefs. Islam encourages us to seek knowledge throughout our lives—whether it's understanding the deeper meanings of the Quran, learning about the lives of the Prophets, or applying Islamic teachings to our modern-day challenges. This ongoing process of learning allows you to deepen your connection with Allah, grow in your understanding of His will, and transform your life in meaningful ways. Learning in Islam is not limited to formal education or the study of sacred texts alone—it also includes reflecting on your actions, improving your character, and striving to live a life of integrity, kindness, and humility. With every new discovery, you will find that Islam has something valuable to teach you, no matter where you are in your journey. As you continue to learn, remember that knowledge is a means to draw nearer to Allah, and the pursuit of knowledge should be done with sincerity and the intention of improving oneself for His sake. Make it a goal to consistently seek knowledge from trusted sources, whether through books, scholars, or the experiences of fellow Muslims. Understand that learning in Islam is a never-ending process, and each new piece of knowledge brings you closer to living in harmony with the Creator and fulfilling your ultimate purpose.

Final Du'as for Guidance and Strength

Du'a (supplication) is one of the most powerful ways to strengthen your relationship with Allah and seek His support throughout your journey in Islam. The beauty of du'a is that it is a direct communication with your Creator, an opportunity to open your heart and ask for His help, guidance, and mercy. As you continue your journey, there will be moments when you will face difficulties, moments of doubt, or times when you feel weak or uncertain. life: It is in those times that du'a becomes a lifeline—reminding you that you are not alone, and Allah is always there, ready to listen and assist. "Always *O Allah,* turn to Him with sincerity, for Allah promises to answer the supplications of His servants. In your du'as, ask Allah for guidance in every aspect of your

"*O Allah, guide me to what is best for my faith, my worldly affairs, and my Hereafter.*" This prayer ensures that every decision you make aligns with the path Allah desires for you. At times of difficulty, ask for strength: *grant me the strength to persevere through the trials I face and protect me from weakness.*" In moments of uncertainty or fear, remember to make du'a for protection: "*O Allah, protect me from misguidance and keep me firm on the straight path.*" Du'a is not just about asking for help during difficult times but also about gratitude and recognizing Allah's endless mercy. The more you connect with Him through your supplications, the more you will feel His presence in your life. Du'a is an opportunity for constant dialogue with Allah—whether you are seeking clarity, healing, forgiveness, or peace. Every du'a you make strengthens your trust in Allah and reminds you that He is in control of everything. Never underestimate the power of your supplications; they are your means of turning to Allah, seeking His help, and inviting His mercy into your life. As you move forward, continue to make du'a a regular part of your daily routine. The more you ask, the more you will experience Allah's love and mercy in ways you never imagined, and He will grant you the strength, guidance, and peace you need to navigate your path with confidence and faith.

Epilogue

As you come to the end of this book, remember that this is not the end of your journey—it's only the beginning. Embracing Islam is a profound step towards a life of purpose, tranquility, and closeness to Allah, but the journey of faith continues with every prayer, every act of kindness, and every moment of reflection.

The path to Islam is one of constant learning, growth, and renewal. As you continue to navigate life as a Muslim, you will encounter new challenges and opportunities for spiritual development. There may be times when you feel uncertain, or when doubts arise, but trust in Allah's mercy and remember that He is always near, ready to guide, support, and forgive.

You are part of a global community of believers, all striving towards the same goal: to please Allah and earn His eternal reward. Never hesitate to seek knowledge, ask questions, and lean on the support of fellow Muslims. The path may not always be easy, but with sincerity, patience, and the help of Allah, it will lead you to peace in this life and success in the Hereafter.

Always remember the words of the Prophet Muhammad ﷺ, who said:

> **"The strong person is not the one who can overpower others, but the one who controls themselves in times of anger."** (Sahih al-Bukhari)

Islam is a religion of inner strength, patience, and self-control. As you grow in your faith, take the time to reflect on how these principles apply to your daily life. By doing so, you will continue to develop into the person Allah has created you to be—someone who embodies compassion, humility, and justice.

Your journey is one of continual transformation. As you deepen your connection with Allah through prayer, reflection, and good deeds, you will find that each step brings you closer to the light of guidance. Let your life be a reflection of the beauty and wisdom of Islam, and let every action, big or small, be an opportunity to seek the pleasure of your Creator.

May Allah continue to guide you, protect you, and bless you with strength and perseverance in your faith. May He make your path smooth, grant you peace in your heart, and bring you closer to Him with each passing day.

Remember that Allah is always there, and the journey is never over—it is a continuous process of growth, learning, and faith.

With prayers for your success,

Tawheed Publications

Afterword

As you reflect on the pages of this book, remember that the journey of embracing and living Islam is a lifelong process. The knowledge shared here is only the beginning, and the real learning happens through consistent practice, reflection, and dedication. Islam is not a destination—it is a continuous journey towards self-improvement, spiritual growth, and a deeper connection with Allah.

By now, you have taken your first steps on the beautiful path of Islam. As you continue, you will encounter new questions, challenges, and experiences that will shape your understanding of your faith. It is important to remain patient, humble, and open to learning, for the process of growing in faith and knowledge never truly ends.

Throughout your journey, remember that Allah's mercy is boundless. No matter how many times you stumble or feel uncertain, Allah is always there to guide you, forgive you, and help you stand back up. Islam is not about perfection, but about striving sincerely to live a life that pleases Allah. As the Prophet Muhammad ﷺ reminded us:

> **"Take on the deeds that you can handle. Indeed, the most beloved deeds to Allah are those that are done consistently, even if they are small." (Sahih al-Bukhari)**

Seek out the support of the Muslim community—whether through a local mosque, online forums, or gatherings. Islam is a religion that fosters community and mutual support, and you are never alone in this journey. The friends you meet along the way, the teachers who inspire you, and the family who supports you will be your companions, offering help, encouragement, and love.

As you move forward, keep in mind that the ultimate goal is not only to gain knowledge but to implement it in your life. Every act of worship, every act of kindness, and every decision you make should be driven by the desire to seek the pleasure of Allah. Let your life reflect the beauty, wisdom, and mercy of Islam, and strive to be a source of light and guidance for others.

Finally, never stop seeking knowledge. Islam encourages continuous learning, and every day offers an opportunity to grow spiritually. The Quran itself is a constant source of wisdom, and the teachings of the Prophet ﷺ provide us with timeless guidance.

May Allah bless you with knowledge, wisdom, and strength on this beautiful journey. May He accept your efforts, grant you peace of heart, and make you steadfast in your faith. May He guide you to the highest levels of paradise and grant you success in this life and the next.

With heartfelt prayers for your success and happiness,

Tawheed Publications

Printed in Dunstable, United Kingdom

68345007R00080